Mastering What You Practice:

Learning to Control Your Emotions

Christian Conte, Ph.D.

ISBN: 9781729526934
ISBN-13: 9781729526934

DEDICATION

To everyone who reads this:
May these words and the effort you put into learning about yourself bring you
much peace.

CONTENTS

ACKNOWLEDGMENTS

Thank you to everyone at Muncy State Correctional Institution for welcoming me and giving me the opportunity to share my Yield Theory with you. A special thanks to Deputy Nicole McKee and Superintendent Wendy Nicholas for their confidence in me and support in my approach from day one. Thank you to my wife and daughter for having to endure far too much time of me being away from home to make this project happen. Finally, a huge thank you goes to the mistakes I've made in my life. Without the mistakes I've made in my life, I never would have learned the little bit that I now know.

HOW TO USE THIS WORKBOOK

You can use this workbook in any way that you want. There are 52 exercises, however, so you could do one exercise a week for one year. If you do one exercise a week, that will give you an opportunity to sit with the lesson that's presented, and then practice implementing it that week. All of the exercises are designed to help you continuously learn about yourself. In other words, you can do the same exercise over and over and get different results, depending on where you are in your life at the time that you do the exercise.

There is a consistent theme throughout this book: You will master whatever you practice, you cannot control the outside world, and your best shot at finding peace is through mastering your own emotions, not through trying to control the outside world. The more you learn about yourself, the more you will have a better sense of why you do the things you do. The more you understand, the better chance you have to use the most helpful strategies possible to handle whatever obstacles you encounter in life.

Group leaders who are intentional with the groups that they lead are more effective than group leaders who have no intention behind what they are doing. Having a workbook like this with 52 different exercises gives group leaders a chance to lead each group they run with a theme. The more intentional group leaders are, the more group members will be able to gain from their groups. So to all group leaders: Use this workbook in the way that best supports your intention for any personal growth group that you run.

For individuals who are not currently part of a group, but are picking this workbook up on their own to seek self-awareness and personal growth: It's important for you to know that you can go through this workbook as quickly or as slowly as you would like. It's wise to understand, however, that there is a difference between understanding a concept intellectually and actually being able to implement that concept in your daily life. Knowing is one thing; doing is often an entirely different thing. It's better to use this workbook in a way that actually helps you live these concepts out, than it is for you to just be able to say that you "did the exercises." In other words, you will get out of this what you put into it.

To everyone who uses this workbook, it's important to remember this: Your ego will try to tell you that you "already know" whatever is being presented to you, but the more you focus on telling others (or even yourself) what you "already know," the less you will focus on using the information to actually find peace. To the best of your ability, try to set your ego aside and go through this workbook with a willingness to learn new things about your incredibly deep and vast mind. Your mind is amazingly complex and wonderful, but your ego doesn't want you to explore all the unknown areas - so it tries really hard to tell you that you already have the answers and that you don't need to learn anything new. Your true self (or the essence of who you are), however, is humble and excited to explore your inner world, and it wants to learn everything it can about the only person you will ever always live with: You.

Willingness to learn + being open to feedback = Knowledge

Using the knowledge you have in your everyday life = Wisdom

Peaceful thoughts + peaceful actions = Peace

INTRODUCTION

You master what you practice. Whatever you practice enough, you master. You feel emotions every day of your life. You also feel an impulse at some point during every day of your life. So you experience emotions and impulses every single day of your life (and as long as you're alive, you always will), and you master whatever you practice in life. But, and here are the real questions that drive this workbook: How often do you take time to practice the way you experience your emotions? How often do you practice the way you respond to your impulses? How often do you practice the kind of peace that you want to feel?

The path to peace isn't complicated. The path to peace does, however, take effort to travel. Deep down inside, you already know what to do to bring yourself peace, but you, like me, and everyone else on this planet, get distracted from the truth you hold in the depths of you. When you allow yourself to be distracted, you forget to practice the things you know to practice. Sure, in this workbook you will learn some new tools - new exercises that you can take with you into your future practice; sure, also, will you learn some new ideas that you can immediately start to put into place in your life - but more importantly than the new ideas and tools this workbook presents, you will be invited to tap into your own internal wisdom. You will be encouraged at every turn to look inward for answers. The more you look inward, the more empowered you are to do what you not only know is right for you, but also what you are absolutely capable of doing.

> A fish once sat in a pond. The pond was old, the creatures in the pond were old, too. The creatures, the objects in the pond, and even the pond itself seemed to be stuck in its ways. But the fish was unique. The fish knew there was more to it all, so she searched inward for answers. The fish never left the pond, but her mind was limitless, and it traveled anywhere she wanted it to go. The fish learned everything she could learn, she talked to every creature who was willing to talk - and everything she learned, everything she thought about, and every conversation she had with herself and others, all led to awareness. The fish eventually learned the greatest secrets of life: *Our outside surroundings cannot determine our inner experience.* Only we are in control of our inner experience. Every moment is an opportunity to learn. Every thought we have and every action we do is practice, and finally: **We master what we practice**.

In many ways, the fish learned what you already know: That life can be difficult at times. But the beautiful lesson the fish learned in the midst of all the difficulties she faced, however, is that, no matter the fact that she was stuck in that old pond, the reality was that her life constantly presents incredible opportunities for her to learn and grow. Wisdom can come from anyone, anywhere, and come at any time. Because of her perspective, and because of what she practiced in her mind every day: This fish eventually found peace.

Like the fish in the story above, you cannot control the vast, outside world, but you can - with practice - control your limitless internal world. Just as you have mastered what you've practiced so far to this point in your life, you can master anything you want with enough practice. The greatest truths in life are not complicated, but they often take effort to discover. The following anecdote is an example of "simple-to-find doesn't always mean simple-to-have."

"Where is peace?" the young girl asked the wise old teacher.

"It is a straight shot down this road," the teacher replied.

"But that is so far!" said the girl, complaining.

"Yes," replied the teacher, "but if you go anywhere else, you will not experience peace."

So the girl, telling herself that it wasn't "fair" that peace was so far off, decided to take herself down different paths for many years. Each path she took brought her pain and emotional unrest. Finally, many years later, she decided to set out to find peace again, and again, she ran into that old wise teacher. "Which way is it to peace?" she asked.

The old, wise teacher smiled lovingly at her and said, "It is a straight shot down this road."

This time, even though the girl saw how far it was, she realized the more time she spent complaining about how far it was, the less time she'd give herself to get there; so without another word of complaint, she immediately set out on the road to peace.

The road to peace is down a straight path, but you have to actually go down that path in order to get there. The road to peace involves you practicing being aware of what you say to yourself and others. It also involves you doing the right thing, and owning complete responsibility for every single thing you say and do. The road to peace involves you practicing the kind of peaceful habits that will actually lead you to a place of peace. The more you practice peace, the better you get at it.

I wrote this workbook because I want to give you an opportunity to learn how to practice the type of habits that lead to peace, because the reality is: I sincerely wish you peace. I realize, however, that no matter how much peace I wish you or wish for you, the eternal truth is that you alone are in control of practicing the type of internal dialogue that can lead you to finding peace.

A teacher once put a bucket in front of each of his students. He told the students to put whatever they wanted into their buckets. Some students put food in their buckets, some put money, and still others put phones inside. The teacher then said, "Whatever you have in your bucket is now in your bucket, right?" And the students agreed (although they looked puzzled at why their teacher would teach them something so obvious). One student even said, "No duh! Whatever we put in our buckets is obviously in our buckets now," and she laughed at the teacher and rolled her eyes. Some of the other students laughed, too.

Then the teacher said, "It seems pretty obvious that whatever you put in your bucket is now in your bucket… And the same is true for your mind. Whatever you put in your mind will be in your mind. So if you fill your mind with violence and anger, you will have violence and anger in your mind. And if you fill your mind with peace, you will have peace in your mind."

The students all understood. The lesson was powerful: Whatever you fill your mind with will be in your mind.

You have time every day of your life. What you choose to put in your mind is up to you. If you watch violence and read violence, then do not expect to for your mind to be magically filled with peace. But if you fill your mind with self-awareness, compassion and peace, then you will have self-awareness, compassion and peace. This workbook is an opportunity for you to fill your mind with the type of information that will ultimately lead you to peace. The words are here; how you choose to take them in now is entirely up to you.

ESSENTIAL WISDOM

There are certain core teachings that I bring to the groups I run, classes I teach, and individual sessions I have. I call it, "Essential Wisdom," because I really believe that these concepts are necessary for helping you find peace.

- **You will master whatever you practice.** If you practice a skill, you will master it. If you practice being angry, you will master that, too. If you practice complaining, you master that. Whatever you practice, you master; but, and this is also true: It's never too late to master something new. So even if you've gotten really good at acting impulsively, it's never too late to start practicing (and mastering) self-control. It's wise to always be mindful that you will master whatever you practice.

- **Your mind always wants to match your body.** In other words, if your body feels anxious, your mind will race to create a story to match what your body is feeling. If your body feels agitated, your mind will quickly search to find a "reason" for why you feel the way you do; and most of the time, that "reason" your mind creates involves something someone else says or does. The more you understand that your mind wants to match your body, the more you can learn how to avoid creating a story to match how your body feels.

- **There is a beginning, middle and end to every emotional situation.** No matter how bad you ever feel, no feeling can last forever. There will be a beginning, middle and end to everything you experience, so it's wise to avoid making an impulsive decision in the beginning or middle of a tough situation that will leave you with a worse ending.

- There is a huge difference between guilt and shame. Guilt is feeling bad about something you've done. Guilt can be a helpful guide to teaching you how to learn from your mistakes. Shame, however, is feeling bad about who you are; and twenty plus years of experience in the field of counseling has taught me that people who live in shame act out of shame. **It's wise to learn how to move beyond shame**, because you are not your actions, and as long as you're alive, you have tremendous opportunities to spread kindness and compassion to others.

- We would rather be angry than anxious or depressed. It actually feels better to lash out in anger than it does to sit in the awful chemicals that are released in anxiety and depression. Unfortunately, after we lash out in anger, we often feel very bad about what we've done, and then we add to the shame we already feel (and remember, those who live in shame act out of shame). **The more you understand how to recognize the anxiety and depression that your body feels, the better chance you have at avoiding lashing out in anger when you're feeling anxious or depressed**. It's wise to be mindful about what's really going on with you.

■ It's perfectly okay to acknowledge or recognize the uncomfortable feelings your body has without reacting to those feelings. **The more you learn how to become the observer of your feelings, the less obligated you will feel to be a puppet to those feelings**. It's wise to remember that every feeling you ever have will eventually pass, so you never need to lash out at others (or yourself) just because you are experiencing uncomfortable temporary emotions.

■ **People see your actions, not your intentions** - so it never matters what you meant to do in life, it only ever matters what you actually do. Interestingly enough, you judge others by their actions, but judge yourself by your intentions. Further, we have a tendency to minimize the pain we cause others, but maximize the pain others cause us. So if you hurt someone, you think, "What's the big deal? I didn't mean to…." But if others hurt you, you think, "I can't believe that person…." The wise understand that people only ever see their actions, not their intentions.

■ There is a difference between what I call the "Cartoon World," or, *the-world-the-way-you-think-it-should-be*, and the "Real World," or, *the world-the-way-it-is*. **The world is not supposed to operate according to how you think it "should," it operates the way it does**. The more you expect others and the world to be what you demand they "should" be, the more you will be let down. The more you learn to align your expectations with the reality of how others and the world actually are, the more peace you will find. The wise understand the difference between the unrealistic demands they make in their Cartoon Worlds and the reality of the world the way it actually is.

■ Your mind experiences somewhere on the order of 50,000 - 70,000 thoughts a day. There is no reason to allow the people and things that you don't like to occupy the majority of your thoughts. After all, the thoughts you have impact the way you feel: So **the more you concentrate on the things you don't like, the more miserable you will be**. Conversely, **the more you concentrate on peaceful thoughts, the more you will fill your mind with peace**. The wise understand that your mind will be filled with whatever you put in it; so be mindful to fill your mind with the type of thoughts that you actually want to be in your mind.

■ You cannot look at exercise equipment and magically get in shape. You have to actually use the equipment and exercise if you want to get in shape. Similarly, you are not entitled to have peace without practicing peace. This workbook (and many books like it) will offer you opportunities to practice peace - but you will not magically experience internal peace until you work hard at practicing the type of skills that lead to internal peace. **The wise understand that they cannot control the outside world and that they cannot always determine what happens to them in life; but, they can always control how they respond to what happens to them in life**.

To begin, let's start here: **Clear goals are much more likely to be met than unclear goals**. You are more likely to reach a destination when you know where you're going. You are wherever you are right now in life. You cannot get one second of the past back, but you can take control of how you handle the present moment, and that in turn will impact your future.

Where are you right now in your life (in terms of where you are physically, mentally and spiritually)?

_____

_____

_____

_____

Where do you want to be (physically, mentally, and spiritually)?

_____

_____

_____

_____

What are you willing to do to get yourself to where you want to be?

_____

_____

_____

_____

You have everything you need to make all the changes you want to make in your life. Now it's time to begin practicing taking complete control of the only thing you can control in life:
You!

MASTERING WHAT YOU PRACTICE

You will master whatever you practice in life. If you practice playing the piano, you will master that. If you practice swimming, you will master that. If you practice acting on your impulses, you will get very good at that, too. BUT, and this is important to know: If you practice peace, you will eventually master that. Many times you don't even realizing what you're practicing. In this exercise, it's important to bring awareness to both what you're practicing and what you want to practice. The more you practice awareness, by the way, the better you get at that, too.

1. Give an example of a time when you practiced snapping at others impulsively in anger.

_____

_____

_____

_____

2. Give an example of a time when you practiced a skill in your life.

_____

_____

_____

_____

3. Give an example of a time when you practiced a good habit (and what the result of that was).

_____

_____

_____

_____

4. List something in the space below that you want to master in life.

_____

_____

_____

_____

5. What is something you can do every single day to help you practice getting good at what you wrote for number 4?

_____

_____

_____

_____

6. What could get in the way of you practicing what you want to master?

_____

_____

_____

_____

7. How could you get around whatever obstacle you wrote for number 6?

_____

_____

_____

_____

"Make an effort to become fully aware of everything that you practice."

SELF-COUNSELING

The best counselor you can ever see is you. You are the only one in the world with complete, unfiltered access to your internal world. And perhaps more importantly, you are the only one in the world who can actually change your thoughts around. You are definitely the only one who can control your behaviors. In this exercise, let's look at what a counseling session would look like *if you were your counselor*.

So, imagine that you came to see a counselor, only to find out that *you* are that counselor. The following is what a counseling session between you and you:

You the counselor: So what are you struggling with right now?

You, client: (Answer)

_____

_____

_____

_____

You, the counselor: So what have you been doing to try to get through that?

You, the client: (Answer)

_____

_____

_____

_____

You, the counselor: Do you feel like that's working? If it is, write down what's working. If it isn't write down why you believe what you're doing isn't working.

You, the client: (Answer)

_____

_____

_____

_____

You, the counselor: If what you're doing honestly isn't working, then what do you think you can do differently? And don't tell me "nothing," because, remember, I am you! So I know that you know there are other things you can try. So what do you think they are?

You, the client: (Answer)

_____

_____

_____

_____

You, the counselor: You are way more capable of solving your struggles than you give yourself credit for being. I'm confident in you. Keep working. Keep searching your mind for solutions. The path to peace isn't always easy, but it is possible.

Conclusion:

Like most people, you can give advice to others more easily than you can live out your own advice. But the reality is, giving advice is significantly easier than living it. It's not that you don't know what to say to yourself to solve your challenges: It's that you don't always *feel* like doing what you know is best for you.

You know what to do and probably even how to do it, but now it's time to do it.

Oh, and the great thing about seeing yourself as a counselor? You are always available on call for yourself 24 hours a day, 7 days a week, every single day of the year!

"Knowing what to do is easier than doing it, but it's only in doing it that you will find the kind of internal peace you want most."

-Dr. Christian Conte

3

ONE WAY OUT

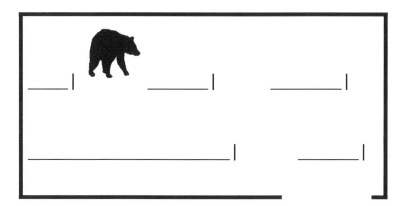

A bear was stuck in a maze. There was only one way out of the maze. The bear was frustrated being in the maze, but one reason she kept getting more and more frustrated was that she kept thinking that there was more than one way out. The truth was, however, there was only one way out, AND, the maze was not complicated at all – there were only 5 obstacles. Now the bear had a choice: Sit in the same spot *wishing that there was another way out* of the maze – OR – *keep moving forward*.

The bear, this very capable, strong bear – she thought about it for awhile. She tried to think of every other way possible to get out of the maze except for going forward, *but **there was no other way out***. Then, an eagle came flying over to talk to the bear. The eagle told the bear that there really was no other way out. The eagle told the bear that he had seen all directions of the maze – (and the truth really was that the eagle had seen the entire maze).

Thank goodness that the bear trusted the eagle. And because the bear trusted the eagle, she decided to keep moving forward. So that's what she did. She moved forward, and because she was so strong and so capable, she actually got through all 5 obstacles and successfully made it out of the maze!

You know exactly what you need to do to get to where you want to be in life. Yes, your path has obstacles, and yes, those obstacles might be challenging to conquer, but yes, also, can you figure it out and conquer those obstacles.

1. What obstacles are in front of you right now?

_____

_____

_____

_____

2. What are you doing (even unintentionally) to stop yourself from getting around those obstacles?

_____

_____

_____

_____

3. What can you do to get out of the psychological "maze" that you're currently in?

_____

_____

_____

_____

Sometimes there's only one way out of a situation. When you encounter a situation that has only one way out, do your best to avoid wasting time trying to go in the wrong direction. Sometimes you have to do what you need to do that's best for you, and not necessarily what you feel like doing at the time. Remember, you are always caring for your future self.

4

IMPOSSIBLE

"I can't do it!" she said. "It's impossible!" And she was scared and sad and frustrated beyond belief. She sat alone in her cell. There was no one to even hear her, let alone understand. She had been through so much. She had experienced every emotion possible. She had just about every thought imaginable. In truth, she knew she survived every experience she ever encountered, but still, there was this overwhelming, pressing thought that nagged at her, saying, "It's impossible, I can't do this!"

When you're hurting, hours and minutes can be confused; days and weeks can be, too. In all the disappointments and let downs, in all the ways in which the world and others in it seem to different from what we want them to be, there is one truth that can get you through anything you face: *Nothing is impossible.* You are an incredible testament to the human spirit. You are a triumph and a living example of strength. The truth is that you can achieve more than even you know you can.

In this exercise, your challenge is to turn "impossible" into "I'm possible." Same letters, completely different meaning….

1. What is the most hopeless you ever felt?

_____

_____

_____

_____

2. What thoughts raced through your mind when you felt hopeless?

_____

_____

_____

_____

Your story doesn't end with a sense of hopelessness; in fact, your story is still being told in this very moment. You are entirely capable. You are powerful. You are strong.

A young reporter once interviewed an elderly woman who survived the atrocities of World War II. The young woman asked the Holocaust survivor, "How were you able to find the strength to get through that experience?" The older woman who had survived the Holocaust and survived the horrific events of being in a concentration camp, looked piercingly through the young reporter and said sternly to her, "You don't "find strength" in those moments, you simply do it." In that moment, the young reporter understood the full effect of this older woman's wisdom: Life isn't always easy or what we think it "should be," but we are more capable than we ever dreamed possible.

3. See yourself as completely capable. What thoughts rush through your mind as you see yourself as completely capable?

_____

_____

_____

_____

4. What habits can you practice to reinforce the reality hat you are completely capable, powerful, and strong?

_____

_____

_____

_____

5. What actions can you do that reflect the best of who you are?

_____

_____

_____

_____

"You are more capable than the world knows; you are more capable, in fact, than even you yet fully know."

- Dr. Christian Conte

THE PROBLEM GENERATOR

"Everything's going really well," she said.

"Well, that's unacceptable," came a reply that sounded like it came from a machine.

"But I can't just make a problem up," the woman said, "I really do feel much better."

"Well, that's simply unacceptable," said the machine in a booming voice.

"So it's not okay to feel good?" asked the woman.

"No! There always has to be a problem!" said the machine. And then the woman received an order to go over to the machine. The machine, you see, was called the Problem Generator. The whole purpose of the machine was to make up problems for people to be upset about, even if there was no real problem.

So the woman went over to the machine, inputted her information into the Problem Generator, and the machine did its job. At first, the machine didn't see anything for the woman to be upset about. She really was being honest that she felt better. But the Problem Generator had an advantage: The Problem Generator knew that we are living on a planet that's spinning in a solar system with a sun that's in a galaxy with more than a hundred billion other suns… so you see, there is always something to think about. The Problem Generator's motto was, "If you can't find a problem to worry about, the Problem Generator can help!"

The Problem Generator took this happy woman, and gave her a bunch of possible things to worry about. "What if an asteroid hits the earth?" or "What if I meet someone someday who says something that I don't agree with?" And the Problem Generator came up with many "problems" like this.

But this woman was different. She was mentally strong. Nothing the Problem Generator came up with resonated with her. She refused to accept the problems that the Problem Generator created for her.

The machine started smoking… It didn't know what to do with someone who didn't get all fired up about the problems it gave them to think about. Eventually, the whole machine burst up in flames and was ruined forever.

Then something incredible happened… With the Problem Generator now broken, people no longer just created problems out of nothing. People were free to be grateful for everything they have. People were free to allow themselves to just feel good.

Once the Problem Generator broke, the people of this world became happy and peaceful. Sure, there were times when some tough moments came up, but every time tough moments came up, people were free to figure out solutions to those problems, rather than fixate on them.

And now you and I are free, in a sense, too. Because of this very brave woman who stood up to the Problem Generator, no one in this world has to create unnecessary problems any longer. We are all mentally free.

In the space below, describe at least two times where you created problems unnecessarily in the past.

_____

_____

_____

_____

_____

_____

_____

_____

_____

_____

_____

"The isolated are careful not to make messes that they don't want to eventually clean."

Zen Proverb

LIKE THE RIVER

There is a beginning, middle and end to every emotional experience. Like the river whose water continually flows, your emotions will continually pass, as well. The river doesn't get upset that water flows; it accepts it. Be like the river: accept that your emotions are temporary. It's helpful to know what your emotions look like, so this exercise is to help you get a clear picture of what the beginning, middle and end of your tough emotions looks like.

1. The beginning of my tough emotions look like this:

_____

_____

_____

_____

2. The middle of my tough emotions look like this:

_____

_____

_____

_____

3. The end of my tough emotions look like this:

_____

_____

_____

_____

"Be mindful that your emotions are temporary, but your actions are permanent."

Dr. Christian Conte

WORD ASSOCIATION

Draw a line linking the words on the left with the likely consequences on the right.

Action	Consequence
Lashing out impulsively	Others not wanting to give more
Meditating	Causing unnecessary fights
Talking calmly	Others appreciating you
Being demanding of others	Getting in shape
Not being grateful	Peace
Using extreme language	Getting unnecessarily upset
Using accurate language	Feeling more balanced
Exercising	Others getting angry
Being kind	Screaming match

You can associate running with getting in shape. You can associate playing drums wildly with loud noise. You can associate speeding in a car with getting a speeding ticket. You can associate turning the light switch to "on" with lights coming on. There are many things you can associate. The same is true of your behaviors. If you are kind to others, others will likely appreciate it. If you use extreme language, you will likely experience getting unnecessarily upset. If you meditate regularly, you will likely experience more peace. The less grateful you are, the less likely others will be to want to give you more. The more demanding you are of others, the more you will likely cause unnecessary fights. The more you complain, the less others will want to be around you. The more accurate language you use to describe your world, the more balance you'll have.

There are some very simple associations in life. The more you take time to reflect on what they are, the more thoughtful you can be with what you choose to do moving forward.

YOU ARE RESPONSIBLE FOR YOU

People don't always **do** what you want. People don't always **say** what you want. *Sometimes* people promise you things and, for whatever reason, end up not following through; other times people outright hurt you with what they say or do. The world does not always work out to your favor; BUT, *there are many times when it absolutely does*. There are many times when things do go your way. You are responsible for whether you choose to focus on the things that don't go your way or the things that do go your way.

You are NOT in control of what others say and do.

You are NOT always in control of the things that happen to you.

But no matter what others say or do, and no matter what happens to you in life, here are two facts that are essential to remember:

1. **You are ALWAYS responsible for your actions.**

2. **You are ALWAYS COMPLETELY responsible for how you handle whatever comes your way.**

Yes, things will be difficult. Yes, it can be tough at times to stay in control of your thoughts and actions, but, no matter what happens, even if it's difficult,***you are strong enough and capable enough to get through any difficult situation***. You are responsible for you.

Remember that there is a beginning, middle and end to every emotional situation. No matter what situation comes up, eventually, it will pass. Do your best to avoid making a poor decision in the beginning or middle of the situation that ultimately makes things worse for you down the road. Remember, too, that there is an enormous difference between what you *need* and what you *want*.

People see your actions, not your intentions, so it doesn't ever matter what you "meant to do" in life; it only ever matters what you actually do. Although you judge yourself by your intentions, others can only judge you by your actions. Before you think, "It's not fair that others judge me by my actions," remember that you only judge others on their actions, too.

You are going to run into situations that are "unfair" and not what you want to face. When you do, you will have a choice regarding how you handle that situation. Even though you might not be responsible for the situation that comes up in the future, you will be responsible for how you handle it.

EXERCISE:

Think about a possible situation that you might experience that could potentially get to you in the future — and **then think of how you can handle it two ways**:

- If you were to let **your impulses** take over and handle the situation poorly, what would it look like? (and what regrets would you ultimately have?)

_____

_____

_____

_____

- If you used **your best self-control** to handle the situation instead, what would it look like (and how might you feel about yourself handling the situation well)?

_____

_____

_____

_____

If you could go back and talk to your past self about handling tough situations differently, what advice would you give your younger self?

_____

_____

_____

_____

"The future will inevitably be here; do your best to make the kind of decisions now that your future self will appreciate."

- Dr. Christian Conte

THE NOT-SO-SCARY PIT BULL

Once there was a pit bull who had gone through an awful lot. She was a really great dog – she was strong and awesome, but she had been hurt a lot, especially when she was a puppy. When she was young, people were mean to her. Because she was hurt a lot when she was a puppy, this pit bull grew up believing that she always had to protect herself. She would snarl at others and act very mean, just to scare others off. You see, deep down inside though, she knew she wasn't really scary, but she also believed that if she acted scary, that others would leave her alone, and it would keep her safe – so that's what she did: She growled and lunged and bit at others, just to keep people at a distance.

Throughout the neighborhood, everyone was afraid of this pit bull. People would say that she was the "meanest dog," and they were afraid of her, because she would bark and bite at anyone who came near her. But then one day, a new family moved into the neighborhood. The new family had a chance to come around the corner and catch the pit bull doing something that no one else ever saw this pit bull do: They caught her being nice to a bird who had crashed into a window and hurt her wing! Yes, it's true! The family saw the pit bull being kind and compassionate. They learned in that moment that the pit bull really was a very nice, kind, loving dog who had just been hurt a lot in her life, so she acted mean to protect herself. They saw right through what she tried to show others.

The pit bull realized that the family "caught" her being nice, and she realized that they saw her for who she truly was. At first, the pit bull tried to deny that she was really kind, and she continued to lunge and bite at others. But this family took her in. They were kind to her no matter how she acted. And then one day, it was as if a light when off in the pit bull's mind: She realized that *she no longer had to act mean to protect herself*. She realized that she didn't like being seen as mean anymore.

Now you know as well as I do that habits are hard to break. The pit bull had to learn that too, but it was a lesson she was willing to learn. She started by "catching herself" every time she started to be mean. At first, she could only recognize it, but before long, she actually learned how to change those mean behaviors into kind behaviors. Even though the family always knew that she was a not-so-scary pit bull, once she changed her behaviors, everyone else learned it, too.

EXERCISE:

We are all like that pit bull at times. We push others away or hide how we're really feeling. We convince ourselves that we are protecting ourselves (or others) by pushing others away, but in the end, when we push others away, we end up hurting ourselves (and others) more than what needs to happen. With awareness, you can see that you never need to push others away again.

1. What are some ways that you have pushed others away at times in the past?

_____

_____

_____

_____

2. Now that you are wiser and experience has taught you what works and what doesn't, how can you express hurt as "hurt," rather than expressing it as "anger."

_____

_____

_____

_____

3. What are some advantages of letting others know that you're hurting inside?

_____

_____

_____

_____

People cannot see in your mind, but they can hear your words. The more you accurately describe your inner world to others, the better chance they have to understand what's really going on inside of you.

10

THE ANGRY SLOTH WHO FOUND PEACE

Once there was sloth who was rather lazy. This sloth would get angry when others didn't do things for him. He felt entitled to have whatever he wanted whenever he wanted it, and even though he was slow in a lot of areas of his life, he was really fast to get angry and lose his temper. He would yell and demand things of others, until eventually, all the other creatures around him didn't want to be near him anymore. He pushed everyone away with his actions.

Then one day he felt alone. He wanted to blame others for not being there for him, but the reality was, no one could even hear his complaints, because he had pushed everyone so far away. This sloth eventually realized (I'd like to say "soon realized," but the truth is that it took a very long time for him to realize this) that no one was around to do anything for him anymore, and if he wanted anything done, he had to do it himself.

Instead of complaining anymore, this sloth learned to just do whatever he needed done. He went from being lazy to be being hard working. He realized that it was his fault that others didn't want to be near him because of his actions and the way he just lashed out and blamed everyone for whatever happened to him. He realized that it was his fault that others no longer wanted to do anything for him, and most importantly, he realized that if he wanted peace in this life, it was his responsibility to find it. And so he did.

He worked on his emotions. He worked on his self-talk. He worked on treating others with compassion and kindness and patience. He worked on expressing gratitude constantly. And one thing led to another, and one day, no one knows exactly which day it was, the sloth found himself around others again. This time, however, he treated others with such kindness, compassion and gratitude, that others wanted to be near him. Others wanted to do things for him, but he insisted on doing everything he could do on his own on his own. Of course, he accepted help if he truly needed it, but if he didn't truly need it, he took care of things on his own. And then it happened:

The sloth who used to be angry and miserable and push others away was now happy and content and surrounded with love. And this now lovable, hard-working sloth felt peace.

EXERCISE:

No one likes to hear that they seem "entitled." Yet every time we demand that others do for us, we are acting entitled. Every time we demand that others think what we think, believe what we believe, or act the way we demand that they act, we are being entitled. As tough as it is to face, the more you recognize when your mind is acting "entitled," the easier it is to stop that kind of thinking, and instead focus on demanding less of others, and demanding more of yourself.

To get clear on the things that you might feel entitled regarding, answer the following questions with the first thought that comes to mind:

People should _____

It's not fair when people _____

When it comes to me, people need to _____

People shouldn't _____

What the world owes me is_____

I only complain because _____

I shouldn't have to_____

Now let's get a sense of how others react when you act a certain way:

When I complain, others have a tendency to_____

When I work hard, others look at me like_____

When I take complete responsibility for what I say and do, others tend to:

_____

When I am kind to others, they respond by_____

When I gossip about others, they respond by_____

When I am positive toward others, they tend to_____

The more aware you are of what others do when you act a certain way, the more you can choose to act in ways that lead you to having the kind of interactions that you want.

11

INTERNAL UNIVERSE

We have the incredible ability to build an entire universe inside our minds. The universe we create in our minds can be anything we want it to be. We can have superpowers in our internal world. We can travel at the speed of light or faster, and we can even be in multiple places at once. The human imagination is literally limitless.

Once there was a woman who didn't realize how incredibly powerful her mind was, and she got caught up in internal wars that were going on in her mind. She would be angry and sad about things that happened in the past. She would allow anxiety about the future to take over sometimes – creating almost a battle in her mind.

And then something beautiful happened: She realized that she was in fact in control of this great universe. She realized that she was the only one who could end the wars in her mind. She was the only one who could create an internal universe that brought her peace. And once she realized that she alone was in control of her internal world, something even more amazing happened: She realized *how* to be in control.

She realized that if she created a peaceful heaven in her mind, her mind would become a peaceful heaven. And that's exactly what she did. Anytime sad, angry, or anxious thoughts came to her mind, she would just erase them by actively thinking about her mind as a peaceful heaven. She would say to the universe: "Thank you." She would express gratitude in her mind *for* her mind. She would say thank you for the ability to have control over her thoughts – for the *moments of* peace that she could now create.

And one moment led to another, and each peaceful moment stretched out longer. The more she practiced it, the better she got at it. The better she got at imagining her mind as a place of peace – as a place of light and love – the more her mind, her internal world – actually became a place of peace, light and love.

The more peaceful her mind became, the more peaceful she became. Before long, everyone around her could see the difference in her. No one ever knew why or how she changed. But she did. She knew. She understood that she was the creator of the universe of her mind. And from that moment on, in her mind, she felt free. She felt in control. She felt peace.

EXERCISE:

The more clear picture you have of your own mind, the easier it will you to know your way around it.

1. Describe what the most beautiful, peaceful place in your mind looks like:

_____

_____

_____

_____

2. Describe the kinds of words and phrases that you can use to keep yourself in a good place mentally regardless of what happens all around you.

_____

_____

_____

_____

3. List the words that would be most helpful for you to repeat to yourself as often as possible throughout the day (for example, repeating words like, "loving-kindness" and "peace" and "I'm okay" and "compassion" etc.):

_____

_____

_____

_____

"The words you say to yourself are building the vast universe that exists inside your mind."

- Dr. Christian Conte

THE CASE OF THE BLUE BIRD

Once there was a blue bird who lived in the Pennsylvania woods. When she was a little bird, some of the cardinals in the tree next to her told her that the name of the woods that they lived in was "England," and the little blue bird grew up her whole life believing that she lived in England, when really, she lived in Pennsylvania.

One day, when the blue bird was an adult bird, she met some other birds who moved into her woods, and she told them how they were in "England." But these birds knew that they were in Pennsylvania, so they thought it was interesting that the blue bird insisted they were all in England. At first, the blue bird was angry that the birds "didn't believe her" about where they were, but the truth was that the blue bird, well-meaning as she was, was simply wrong. And even though it wasn't her fault, the fact was: She was not in England. She was in Pennsylvania.

The blue bird was an awesome bird. She was intelligent, strong, and capable; but she did have a very hard time letting go of the belief that she was in England. And there really was nothing wrong with her believing that she was in England, except for one tiny, but pretty important fact: She was actually in Pennsylvania.

QUESTIONS

1. If you were talking to the blue bird, and you wanted to help her understand that she was in Pennsylvania, not England, how would you go about helping her understand that?

_____

_____

_____

_____

2. How would you respond to the blue bird if she got angry with you for not "believing" her, even though you know that her belief is inaccurate?

_____

_____

_____

_____

3. Would it be better for you to just let the blue bird believe that she's in England, and then just not take what she says seriously? Or would it be better for you to try to help her understand where she actually lives? (Explain your answer)

_____

_____

_____

_____

There will be times in your life when you meet others who seem to struggle with seeing the reality of the world, and you will have to decide if, when, and how you will approach that person. There could be times, too, when you struggle with the way you are seeing the world; and in those moments, you will have to ask yourself if can draw on the courage it will take to allow yourself to be humble and listen to what others are seeing. None of us will be right about everything in life, and those who try to be right about everything will likely run into many problems along the way.

Do your best to put your ego aside at all times. It takes great strength to set your ego aside. The more you can set your ego aside, however, the more strength you will exude, and the more humble you will be in those moments. From a place of humility and strength, it is easier to listen openly to the perspective of others.

There is an old saying that goes, "You can be right or you can be happy, but you cannot be both." Now maybe that saying is true and maybe it's not, but experience sure tells us that very few people want to hang around anyone who has a hard time admitting when she's wrong. Imagine the gravestone that says, "Here lies Sally Smith. No one liked being around her. She died alone and miserable, but she was right 13,987,245 times in her life." Being right might make your ego feel good temporarily, but it can sometimes come back to hurt you in the end.

If one person tells you something one time, it might not be true; but if more than one person tells you the same thing (or even if one person tells you the same thing multiple times), then there's a very good chance that what they're seeing is true, and you simply cannot see it. Just as we can see what's going on with others more easily from the outside, others can see what's going on with us from the outside, as well.

"Be open to feedback. Others can often see you more accurately than you can see yourself."

- Dr. Christian Conte

THE COST OF DISTRACTION

A lot of times you might find yourself cruising through life on autopilot. Sometimes that's perfectly fine; but other times, your "automatic" thoughts might be getting to you or causing you grief in some way. In those moments, it's wise to step back and **pay attention to what you think and what you do**. The cost of distraction is sometimes more than we are willing to pay. Because of that, it is often worth your effort to be mindful of what you're saying to yourself, especially when your body feels "off" in some way.

In this exercise, take some time to reflect on the types of thoughts and actions that lead you to places you would rather not be. Once you know how you got there, it will be easier to leave those places.

1. When I start to feel anxious, these are the types of thoughts I have:

_____

_____

_____

_____

2. When I start to feel anxious, these are the types of behaviors I do:

_____

_____

_____

_____

3. When I start to bring myself out of anxiety, these are the types of thoughts I have:

_____

_____

_____

_____

4. When I start to bring myself out of anxiety, these are the types of behaviors I do:

_____

_____

_____

_____

5. When I find myself wanting attention in a negative way, these are the types of thoughts I have:

_____

_____

_____

_____

6. When I find myself wanting attention in a negative way, these are the types of behaviors I do:

_____

_____

_____

_____

7. When I find myself wanting attention in a positive way, these are the types of thoughts I have:

_____

_____

_____

_____

8. When I find myself wanting attention in a positive way, these are the types of behaviors I do:

_____

_____

_____

_____

9. When I allow my mind to run wild, these are the kinds of thoughts that I have:

_____

_____

_____

_____

10. When I feel truly peaceful inside, these are the kinds of thoughts that I have:

_____

_____

_____

_____

Being aware of what you think and what you do can help you catch yourself in the future when you start to think and do things that are not helpful for you. The more you know what works for you, too, the easier it will be for you to get to that space in the future. Just as sure as you know that $1 + 1 = 2$, you also know that what you think directly impacts how you feel. The more you tell yourself peaceful thoughts, the better you get at telling yourself peaceful thoughts. The better you get at telling yourself peaceful thoughts, the better you get at mastering peace.

14

ROCK AND A HARD PLACE

Anytime you don't feel good on the inside, it's natural to want to lash out at others; but just because it's natural that you might feel like lashing out at others doesn't mean that you should. In fact, personal growth is all about becoming more aware of yourself and why you do the things you do; and it's also about making the changes you need to make. Just because something is understandable doesn't mean it's right to do.

Have you ever been around others who are struggling so much on the inside that they put you between a rock and a hard place when they talk to you? In other words, they ask you questions in such a way that you're wrong in their eyes if you say "yes," and you're wrong if you say "no." And if you try saying "maybe," or if you try to avoid answering them altogether, they *still* get upset with you. When people put you between a rock and a hard place, you are wrong no matter what you do. If you've ever experience people putting you between a rock and a hard place, you know it's a very tough place to be.

Of course, we're all human, and we all mess up from time to time. We all make mistakes. Our goal is to keep learning about ourselves and keep getting better all the time. So in this exercise, the aim is to think about times when *you* have put others between a rock and a hard place.

1. Give an example of a time when you put someone between a rock and a hard place. (In other words, you were ready to be mad at them no matter what they said.)

_____

_____

_____

_____

2. Thinking back on that situation, describe the hurt you were feeling inside that led you to want to lash out at that person.

_____

_____

_____

_____

3. In retrospect, what could you have done differently instead of putting others between a rock and a hard place?

_____

_____

_____

_____

15

THE BIGGEST DRAMA EVER!

"I'm writing a play," the screenwriter said, "and I want to make it the biggest drama ever!"

"Oh please let me help you write it!" said her friend.

"Okay, definitely!" replied the screenwriter. And the two of them got right to work.

Here's what they came up with:

ACT I

A captain walks into room in a where a group of soldiers are sitting.

"Oh my goodness!" exclaimed the first soldier, "Did you see that? I can't believe it! She didn't even say 'hello' to me! I know she hates me!"

"Wait," said another solider, "You mean she really didn't say 'hello'?"

"Yes!" the first soldier replied, "I'm serious! This is the worst day ever!"

"Well, what if you were dying?" asked the third solider. "You could have been dying, and she didn't even say 'hello'?"

"That's what I was thinking!" said the first solider. "Wait, are you stealing my thoughts?" she asked angrily.

"Oh my goodness," said the second solider, "She is NOT stealing your thoughts! You don't know what you're talking about!"

And the room erupted in chaos. One solider after another complained about how her problems were the worst and that no one could ever understand what she's been through. And each solider tried to top the other. And each solider said, "I don't try to top anyone!" And, "I'm not like the rest of them," but in reality, all the soldiers acted the exact same way. They made giant mountains out of even the smallest molehills. They used words like, "Everybody!" and "Nobody!" and "Always!" and "Never!" and whatever happened to them, they made a thousand times bigger than it actually was. Everything was exaggerated. Everything was made out to be the end of the world. All of the soldiers were exhausting to be around, because nothing was ever enough for them, and none of them was ever satisfied with anything. In fact, even if a problem didn't exist, they'd create one.

The whole place was emotionally draining, because the exaggerations were endless. The screenwriter and her friend stopped after they finished Act I, and they decided to write the same Act over, except this time without drama - just so that they could see how good they could really learn what makes something actually filled with drama.

Here's what it looked like:

ACT I (re-written)

A captain walks into a room where a group of soldiers were sitting.

"She didn't say 'hello' to me," said the first soldier.

"Um," replied the second soldier, "You know there could be a million reasons for that. Don't take it personally."

"Ha," laughed the first soldier, "I was just joking. I know there are a million reasons for that, I was just thinking how funny it would be if I read more into it than was actually there."

"Yeah," said the third soldier, "It would be really unfortunate if any of us ever read into situations more than was actually there."

"I think the reality is," said the first solider, "that what we see in the outside world is merely a reflection of what's going on inside of us."

"That's so true," said the second soldier.

And they went on to have conversation about the balance in the universe. They talked about how things seem to happen for a reason, even if we can't pinpoint the reason at the time. And they talked about how empowering it is to learn from every moment. They talked about how great it feels to not make assumptions, not act on impulses, and to practice self-control. *They used accurate language when they spoke*, and they noticed how they were similar to each other in many ways. They talked about how learning self-control took them practice, but the practice was worth their effort. They talked about the feeling of peace they get from being able to avoid exaggerating things. They talked about their dreams and goals and were mindful to focus on the big things in life to avoid getting caught in the little things. Their speech to each other was kind. Their experience of life was peaceful.

The lessons that the screenwriters learned:

We make mountains out of mole hills and create drama any time that we:

*   Read more into situations (especially with negative assumptions)

*   Take things personally

*   Use exaggerated language that simply isn't accurate

EXERCISE:

The key to learning and personal development is to understand that we all do things ineffectively from time to time, and we can all constantly improve. In this exercise, think about the story of The Biggest Drama Ever! and answer the following questions:

1. What are the primary differences between Act I written two different ways?

_____

_____

_____

_____

2. In what ways have you created drama where none existed in the past?

_____

_____

_____

_____

3. In what ways have you made a "mountain out of a mole hill" in the past?

_____

_____

_____

_____

4. If you could go back and talk to yourself at the time when you were making a mountain out of a mole hill in the past, how would you coach yourself through that situation so you could handle it more effectively?

_____

_____

_____

_____

5. What can you do to avoid creating unnecessary drama in the future?

_____

_____

_____

_____

6. How have you taken things personally that eventually, you learned weren't personal at all?

_____

_____

_____

_____

7. How have you used exaggerated language (e.g., "always," "never," "can't stand it," etc.) to make things bigger than they actually were?

_____

_____

_____

_____

8. What can you do in the future when your mind begins to make things bigger than they are?

_____

_____

_____

_____

"We master what we practice… whatever we practice."

16

WHAT YOU SEE IS WHAT'S INSIDE

QUESTION: What is the picture above?

ANSWER: There is no correct answer.

What you see in this picture is a reflection of what is inside of you. This picture is like the outside world. The world is what the world is, and how you see it often tells you much more about yourself than it does about anything else. If you're filled with anger, you're more likely to focus on the mistakes others make and/or look for arguments to have. If you're filled with sadness, you will likely look for what is missing in the world. If you're filled with anxiety, you might focus on what could be in the world. If you're filled with courage, you're likely to see every tough experience you have as an obstacle. If you're filled with peace, you're likely to see the goodness all around you.

Here's your challenge in this exercise: Look at the world around you – then, more importantly – Look at your inner thoughts. You cannot control the outside world. You can control your thoughts. Controlling your thoughts is not easy. There's no doubt that controlling your thoughts takes effort and practice, but there's no doubt, also, that it's possible to control your thoughts. Change is possible. Change is always possible.

EXERCISE: Repeat the phrase, "Loving-kindness" to yourself 50 times in a row. Do your best to really think about those words as you say them. After you have said those words about 50 times (the point isn't to say them exactly "50" times, it's to say them a lot), think about how you feel.

The more you fill your inner mind with peace, the more likely you are to see peace in the outside world.

-Dr. Christian Conte

The following page is an example of the type of poster that you can use (or make one that fits you best) and put on your wall. Remember, our surroundings impact us, so the more we can surround ourselves with peaceful sayings, the more likely we are to practice saying them. And of course: We master what we practice.

Fill your mind with the type of thoughts that you want to be in your mind.

The more you repeat loving-kind words and phrases over and over to yourself, the more your mind will be filled with loving-kind thoughts.

Internal peace doesn't happen by accident; it takes effort to have, and it takes effort to maintain.

Be kind in the way that you speak to yourself, because you're listening.

"Your peace is worth your effort."

- Dr. Christian Conte

17

THE FISH WHO FISHED AND THE FISH WHO BIT

There are some really unique fish in the ocean. One species of fish called the "angler" fish actually does some fishing herself. That's right, deep down in the dark depths of places in the ocean well below where any light can hit, there lives a type of fish that has what looks like a fishing rod protruding from its forehead, and at the end of that "fishing line" is a sort of light. What happens is that this "fisherman's fish" baits other, smaller fish to be drawn to the light in the depth of all that darkness, and once the other fish have been sufficiently "baited," this fish strikes and gets her meal.

Sometimes humans "bait" others to bite, too (and not just fish). Consider these examples:

- Person X sends a letter to Person B saying, "I just can't take it anymore…." And then doesn't explain what's going on, so Person B gets worried and wonders what's going on with Person X. Or, at least that's what Person X wants by "baiting" the other person. Person X wants the other person to ask her how she's doing. She wants her to care about her, and instead of just asking for that love and attention in healthy ways, she "baits" the other person to ask about her.

- Person B doesn't respond to what Person Y asks her. Person B is hoping that Person Y will read into her silence and worry about her. In using silence, Person B is "baiting" Person Y to care more about her.

- Person L starts to say that she "might not be here tomorrow," and then won't say more about what's going on or what she means. In this way, Person L "baits" others to ask over and over what she means, and Person L "baits" others to get pulled into her fishing line of drama.

Instead of "baiting" others to find out if they care about you, it's much healthier to simply ask them. "Baiting" others is a game. Asking others if they care is the mature, healthy path to take. Think of instances where you "baited" others to ask more about what was going on with you. How could you have sought their care, their assurance, or their attention in a different way?

_____

_____

_____

_____

How have others tried to bait you into asking more about them?

_____

_____

_____

_____

What does it feel like to have others try to bait you into showing interest in them?

_____

_____

_____

_____

Even though you know deep down that others cannot see your thoughts, there were probably times in your life where you have been upset with others for not "knowing" what was going on inside you. But the reality is that others can only see your actions, not your thoughts. You no doubt have not liked when others were upset with you for not asking about (or knowing about) what was going on with them, so it's wise to avoid doing that to others in the future.

When you "bait" others, you play the helpless victim. The problem with you playing the helpless victim is that you are not helpless. You are strong and capable. Even though there will of course be times in your life where you don't feel especially strong, it's important to remember that you are never "helpless." It's unwise to expect others to magically know what's going on with you. Be mindful to express what you want in the clearest way possible. The fewer games you play, the more likely you are to communicate effectively.

EXERCISE:

Have a discussion about the difference between "being victimized" and "playing the victim." Point of understanding: Although being victimized is a tragedy, playing the victim is a choice.

"You are significantly stronger than you know."

Dr. Christian Conte

18

THE SUPERHERO OF YOUR LIFE

You are the superhero of your life. You have overcome obstacles throughout your entire life. The obstacles you've overcome are honestly what have contributed to you becoming strong. In this exercise, the focus is on *your strengths* and how *you have been able to overcome* them. Give a brief description/general overview of past obstacles you've faced – and then focus primarily on describing specifically what you did to overcome it.

Obstacle #1: _____

HOW I OVERCAME IT:

_____

_____

_____

_____

Remember, there were moments when you first encountered that first obstacle when you believed that you could not overcome it. That's what obstacles do: They try to convince you that you cannot overcome them. But they're wrong. Think of a second obstacle that once seemed really difficult for you to overcome:

Obstacle #2:

HOW I OVERCAME IT:

_____

_____

_____

_____

Like the first two obstacles, you can see a theme emerging: There were moments in your life that you didn't think you would overcome what was in front of you. But., the other common aspect to all obstacles you ever faced in your past is this: You were able to overcome every obstacle you've faced in your past. No matter how difficult, you have actually survived every tough situation you ever encountered. Think of a third obstacle that seemed almost overwhelming at the time:

Obstacle #3:_____

HOW I OVERCAME IT:

_____

_____

_____

_____

No matter what you are facing right now, like every obstacle you have ever faced in your past, you have the ability to overcome. Whatever obstacle you're facing now, think of your future self. Think of who you will be in the distant future. Imagine yourself looking back on this moment, and think of the best possible way to get through anything you're experiencing.

Reminder: Draw on the strengths you have developed already to help you overcome any new challenges you face.

19

HOW YOUR MIND MATCHES YOUR BODY

Your mind will always try to match your body. If your body feels off, your mind will want to create a story to match it. Without even realizing it, our minds create stories to help us make sense of the world, and that starts with us. When you feel anxious, irritable, sad, mad, etc. you mind will want to help you understand why.

Here's how it works:

4. Mind

3. Body

2. Mind

1. Body

The more your body feels bad, the more your mind will race to make sense out of it. We all create narratives or "stories" to make sense out of what's happening inside of us. The more off we feel, the worse our story; the worse our story, the more off we feel. The only way to combat this cycle is to recognize it and ultimately, break it. The more you accept that your body feels off, but there's no need to create a narrative (or story) to match, the better chance you give yourself to get through the moment in the best possible way.

Give an example of a time when your body felt <u>anxious</u> and your mind made up a story to match how your anxious body felt.

_____

_____

_____

_____

Give an example of a time when your body felt <u>irritable</u>, and your mind made up a story to match that feeling of irritability.

_____

_____

_____

_____

Give an example of a time when your body felt <u>agitated</u>, and your mind made up a story to match that feeling of agitation.

_____

_____

_____

_____

Give yourself a clear plan of what you can say to yourself and do the next time your body feels "off" a bit:

_____

_____

_____

_____

The more you can recognize that your mind wants to match your body, the faster you can change that story. It's okay to say to yourself, "I'm okay." The more you tell yourself that you're okay, the more your body eventually believes it. The more you tell yourself that you're "okay" or "safe," the less extreme your body needs to react. And here's a wonderful fact: Your body cannot hold two opposing states at once. In other words, you cannot be simultaneously calm and anxious. Because you cannot be calm and anxious at the same time, if you can work to make your body calm (by saying things to yourself like, "I'm okay," or "I'm safe"), then your mind will follow.

"You are the author of your life: Happy writing!"

Dr. Christian Conte

-

20

MAYBE

Anger arises from certainty. The more certain you are about things, the more upset you'll be when things aren't that way. The more certain you are that people are "out to get you," the more personal you will take anything that comes up. The more you can doubt your certainty, however, the better chance you give yourself to handle things in a rational way. The truth is, after all, that just the way you are more focused on yourself than you are on others, the same is true for others. Human beings are inherently more focused on themselves. And whereas we all have a tendency to expect others to be focused on us more (even though we're not focused on others more), the reality is that people do the things they do largely because all human beings tend to want to maximize their pleasure and minimize their pain. The more you can cast doubt into your certainty that others are "out to get" you, the more peace you will feel.

The following list of "maybes" are designed to help you move away from the certainty that leads to anger, and instead move more into the realm of doubt that leads to peace:

Maybe things are the way I see them, but maybe they're not. Maybe I make things out to be worse than they actually are… maybe.

Maybe I blame others for how I feel a little too often. Maybe.

Maybe I blame others for the things I do, when the truth is, I know that others aren't responsible for what I do: I am.

Maybe the things I'm so certain about aren't really things I should be so certain about…. Maybe….

What if I'm wrong about the way I see the world? What if I have to trust that what others are telling me is more accurate than what my own mind is telling me? Maybe I can't do that…. Maybe.

Maybe I can.

Maybe it's important for me to set my ego aside and listen to others with humility… Maybe….

Maybe what others do really isn't as personal as I seem to be taking it…. Maybe.

Maybe it's okay to not have to exaggerate everything I'm experiencing to get others attention…. Maybe.

Maybe I'm wrong right now. Maybe….

Maybe I am experiencing what's happening to me right now for a reason… Maybe….

Maybe if I doubt my anger more, I will feel less angry…. Maybe….

Maybe I played a bigger role in why I'm in the spot I'm in than I've allowed myself to admit….

Maybe it's time to let go of all the anger I've been holding onto…

Maybe….

"Certainty dwells in arrogance. Doubt lives in humility. Live wherever is best for you."

- Dr. Christian Conte

21

BUILDING PEACE ALL AROUND YOU

Buildings are put together brick by brick, cinder block by cinder block. Every brick, every cinder block, has its own individual story. The bricks, the cinder blocks... they were all forged and built through mixing heat and rough movement. They were each created through sweat and challenge. Every brick, every cinder block tells a story.

Look around you. Look at the bricks or cinder blocks that you can see. Just the way each brick and each cinder block has its own individual story, the same is true for the memories of your life. Just as the bricks and cinderblocks around you create your surroundings, the memories you choose to focus on are the ones that will create your mental surroundings, and that will ultimately dictate how you feel.

You are the architect of your own life. Sure, you've encountered obstacles barriers. Of course there things that have gotten in the way of the way you wanted to build your life. But amongst all the struggles you've experienced, you've also had moments where you overcame.

Look around you again. This time see those same bricks, those same cinder blocks, but this time, you are the architect who will infuse a new element to every brick or cinder block you see. This is your chance to build the mental space around you.

Here's your task:

One by one, brick by brick, take the time to associate a positive memory with each brick or cinder block in your cell. Specifically recall a moment where you had the strength to overcome a tough time or even just a positive memory in general, and then link that memory with a particular brick or cinder block.

Of course as you think back over the memories of your life, you will inevitably recall difficult times. Your challenge in this exercise is to avoid focusing on the difficult parts, and instead focus entirely on how you were able to overcome. This is about you empowering you. And here's some helpful encouragement to think about: You have survived every single difficult experience of your life!

This exercise is your chance to build the walls around you with memories of strength, with memories of the ways in which you have been capable, and with positivity. When you take the time to decorate your cell with positive memories, you will be creating a beautiful mental environment. This is about you building up your own strength. It's about you creating a mental environment that will help you.

Start with one brick or cinder block. Take your time, and infuse a good, positive memory onto that block.

Take your time and put effort into building peace around you. In the space below, describe at least three bricks or cinder blocks, and how in the memories you will associate with that. Remember this is not about the negative memories, but about the way in which you were able to overcome.

This is about strength. This is about you building the walls of your space with strength. Regardless of where you are, *you are always the architect of your mental space*.

Positive memory	Positive memory		Positive memory	
	Positive memory	Positive memory		Positive memory
Positive memory			Positive memory	
	Positive memory			

22

THE BEAR WHO PRETENDED HE WAS SOMETHING HE WASN'T

Once there was a group of woodland creatures who all lived in the same forest. Every week, the animals would get together to have a group meeting. There was a squirrel, a bear, an eagle, a beaver, a groundhog, and a bunny. They would all gather around

Every week, the animals would talk about something that would help them. Every week, one of the creatures, the bear, would seem to be off in the way he talked to the other animals. He would make up words and go off on tangents that were off the subject. The other animals would get frustrated because the bear would talk in circles and make up words. The bear didn't seem to notice though, and even though he didn't really seem to have any real friends among the animals, he was very friendly, nonetheless. He just always seemed to be talking to himself, and he never seemed to be really interested if the other animals got what he was saying or not.

One day an owl came flying into the woods and had a chance to talk with the bear. The owl had a different experience of the bear than all the other animals. The owl realized that the bear was very smart, and the bear actually just liked to pretend that he didn't know what was going on. The owl found out a secret: The bear really was pretending! The bear liked to pretend that he couldn't stay on topic or that he had to throw in made-up words to make others feel like they were confused. The bear was having fun at everyone else's expense.

Well the owl and the bear talked. And the owl didn't judge the bear for what he did. The owl wasn't mad at all. But something shifted in the bear after that, and wouldn't you know, the bear started talking to everyone normally after that. The bear started getting along with the other animals and made lots of friends. The bear and the other animals all lived happily ever after.

Sometimes you and I pretend to be something we're not. Sometimes we start out doing that to protect ourselves, but over time, as you know, whatever we practice, we master. So sometimes, and only sometimes, mind you, we begin practicing being something we're not until we actually become that thing.

No matter what you ever experience, however, and no matter where life takes you or what life shows you: Always remember to come back to your center. At the core of who you are is exactly who you are. And no one and nothing can tell you that you're something you're not - not even you. So give your best effort today, and every day, to be who you know you really are deep down inside.

EXERCISE:

In full disclosure, here is a way that I have pretended to be something I wasn't in the past:

_____

_____

_____

_____

Here is what I wanted people to believe about me at the time:

_____

_____

_____

_____

When I am not being true to myself in the future, here is the way I hope people approach me to help me be aware of what I'm doing:

_____

_____

_____

_____

"Feedback can be hard to take; but living with repeating the same mistakes over and over again from not accepting feedback, however, is even more difficult to take."

- Dr. Christian Conte

23

EMOTION REGULATION

Handling our emotions can be challenging at times, but the more we practice handling our emotions well, the better we get at it. It's easy to lash out at others. It's easy to blame others for how we feel. It's easy to make the impulsive decision. It's tougher to sit with our emotions. It's tougher to sit back and learn from our emotions. It's tougher to not make the impulsive decision. It takes self-discipline to be able to handle our emotions well.

One incredible skill to develop is called "Emotion Regulation." Emotion regulation is a pretty fancy term, but all it means is that we learn how to regulate (or handle) our emotions. So, for example, if you feel anxious or angry and want to act out impulsively, emotion regulation means you work through that and don't lash out. As I have stated many times already: There is a beginning, middle and end to every emotional experience, and no matter what you're going through, it will eventually pass.

Our minds want to match our bodies, so when our bodies start to feel anxious or angry or depressed, our minds will race to make up a story to make sense out of why we feel the way we do. Emotion regulation is understanding that your mind will want to make up a story, and it's having the strength and mental toughness to not make up or go with that story. It's having the self-discipline to sit with that emotion without reacting to it. It's understanding that no matter how tough of a moment it is, it will eventually pass.

You are stronger than you realize. You have the ability to hesitate before acting impulsively. Yes, it takes effort. Yes, it can be tough to do at times; but here's the thing: You are capable of doing it. The more you practice emotion regulation, the better you get at it.

What is the toughest kind of emotion that you experience?

_____

What can you say to yourself to help you get through that tough emotion?

_____

_____

_____

_____

What can you say to yourself that would make that emotion even worse?

_____

_____

_____

_____

What can you say to yourself during that tough emotion that can at least take the sting out of what you're experiencing?

_____

_____

_____

_____

The more you tell yourself that you're "okay" or "safe," the more you start to believe it. You will master what you practice, and that includes the self-talk that you have. *Always be mindful of what you're saying to yourself because you are certainly listening.*

When you feel hurt inside, instead of coming at others and blaming them for how you feel, take some time to reflect on how you can change your thoughts around. After all, you cannot change the outside world, and you cannot change what others say and do, but you can control what you choose to focus on. The next time you feel hurt inside, think about what that hurt is trying to teach you. The more you can learn from your emotions, the more you can grow from every experience.

What you focus on often determines how you feel. When you focus too much on having things go your way, you can get really upset when they don't. When you can focus instead, for example, on giving good energy to the world, then your thoughts can be more centered on compassion and kindness. The more your thoughts are centered on compassion and kindness, the better you will feel inside.

"Every experience, no matter how great or terrible, is an opportunity to learn."

- Dr. Christian Conte

24

PEACE TAKES PRACTICE

Once there were two aliens who came to Earth. Their spaceships landed in two different homes. They landed at the same time in the same way, but each experienced two entirely different reactions. Both aliens landed in homes where the people were willing to teach them the language. Both aliens landed in English speaking homes. But wow! was both of their experiences different.

The first alien landed in a home where the people spoke in extremes. "This is terrible!" the family said. And everything they taught the alien had to do with extreme adjectives. "I can't believe this is our terrible luck!" the people would say, and the alien learned their way. "Nothing's fair!" they would say! "Why did you have to land here?" they would complain. "Now we have to spend our money on feeding you!" they could cry out. The alien soon learned how to complain, too. He learned how to exaggerate everything that happened. He learned how to express discontent with everything. After all, he did not know the language until he met this family.

Ultimately, he learned that he was a terrible bother to the humans, and he felt awful and guilty and terrible. He really disliked this planet, and all he wanted to do was leave. The humans didn't realize that their own words and actions were making him feel awful. they didn't realize that they taught him how to experience Earth, so when he wanted to leave, they simply complained more, "Look how ungrateful aliens are! After everything we did for them, too!" they would say. The alien couldn't wait to leave.

The other alien landed in a home where gratitude was all the family expressed. "Thank you for landing on our home!" they said. "Thank you for showing us that there is life out there!" And the family spoke with gratitude about everything, and the alien in turn, learned how to speak in gratitude. Because the alien learned peaceful dialogue, the alien learned to feel peace. The alien felt welcomed in this home, and hoped to stay forever. The family was happy. The alien was happy. Sure, the world wasn't perfect, but the world's not supposed to be: All we can ever do is hope to talk to ourselves in the way that helps us best.

EXERCISE:

If an alien landed in your space, and you were the one to teach the alien about the world, what would you teach the alien?

_____

_____

_____

_____

By following your teachings, would the alien learn peace or anger and unrest?

_____

_____

_____

_____

What do others learn about the world by watching and learning from the way you experience life?

_____

_____

_____

_____

"You are teaching others, whether you realize it or not: Be mindful what it is others learn by watching you."

- Dr. Christian Conte

25

EXTREME WORDS PRODUCE EXTREME FEELINGS

The words you use _directly impact_ the way you feel. The words you use also have a direct impact on the conversations you have with others.

Here are examples of _unnecessarily extreme descriptions_:

NOBODY listens to me!

(If anyone has <u>ever</u> listened to you in your life, then it is an <u>untrue</u> statement to say that "nobody" ever listens to you....)

We NEVER get support from _____.

(If you have received support from that person or group <u>even once</u> before, then it is <u>untrue</u> and <u>inaccurate</u> to say that you "never" get support....)

You ALWAYS do that!

(If people have <u>even one</u> experience not doing whatever it is that you're telling them they "always" do, then you are <u>unnecessarily</u> using extreme language.)

EVERYONE around here _____.

(If there is <u>even one exception</u> to your statement, then it is not "everybody," and you are using <u>unnecessarily</u> exaggerated language.)

I CAN'T STAND when people _____.

(If you are able to <u>physically stand up</u>, then it is <u>inaccurate</u> to say that you "cannot stand" something.)

The more extreme words you use in your self-talk, the more extreme and intense emotions you will feel. The more extreme words you use with others, the more defensive they become. Remember, <u>you are only in control of you</u>, so do your best to be mindful to avoid using extreme language. At a minimum, try your hardest to at least _catch yourself_ if you do use extreme words (such as: "everyone," "nobody," "always," "never, ""can't stand it," etc.). The more aware you are of the words you use, the better chance you have to change them. The more accurate your language, the more balanced you'll feel.

EXERCISE:

Give an example of a time you used extreme words to describe your situation, when, looking back on it, you see now that the adjectives you used were a bit extreme:

_____

_____

_____

_____

Give an example of an upcoming situation that might happen where you can replace the old way you used to experience situations with a new calmer (and accurate) description of what's going on:

_____

_____

_____

_____

Just for fun, describe the following situation in two different ways. In the first way, use extreme words (like, "I can't stand this!"), and in the second way, use more accurate language (like, "I don't like this, but I can handle it.").

First way (EXTREME LANGUAGE). Someone tells you that you cannot have something you ask for (use extreme words to describe not getting what you want):

_____

_____

_____

_____

Second way (ACCURATE LANGUAGE). Someone tells you that you cannot have something that you ask for (this time, use accurate language to describe not getting what you want):

_____

_____

_____

_____

Situations will come up your entire life where things don't go your way. When things don't go your way, you can look at it many different ways. One way you can look at it is this: If it already didn't go your way, then why use extreme adjectives to make yourself feel worse? Or another way you can look at it is: If things didn't go your way, then why not use accurate language like, "It's not the end of the world, I can handle it," to help yourself handle the situation more effectively? At the end of the day, the world will not always give you what you want, but the more you use accurate language to describe what happens, the more likely you are to find balance in your life.

"You cannot always change the outside world, but you alone have access to the way you describe the way you experience the outside world."

- Dr. Christian Conte

FINDING PEACE IN GRATITUDE

Once there was a woman who was having a tough day. All day long she thought about things that upset her. She found herself upset about the past or worrying about the future. The whole day long, the only place her mind would be was somewhere else – the past or the future. And then the worse she felt, the more she found herself making a bigger deal out of things that really weren't that big of a deal. In fact, to that point in the day, she just didn't feel like herself - and she just couldn't figure out why. And then, all of a sudden, it happened….

Her mind left the past and came back from the future: She became fully involved in the present moment. In the present moment, ***she felt gratitude***. She felt gratitude for her breath. She felt gratitude for her eyesight (she really appreciated being able to see colors). She felt gratitude for her arms and legs (she felt gratitude that she could move them). She felt gratitude for the present moment. The feeling of gratitude overcame her so much that the only thing she felt was peace.

And then she began to almost see gratitude. She saw gratitude all around her. She looked for it. She noticed it. And then she began to express it. She began to thank people around her for even the most basic things. The more she thanked people, the more she spread gratitude, the more she spread peace. Soon, she found herself in an entirely different place: A place of peace.

On top of finding peace in the present moment, she also figured out how to hold onto that feeling longer and longer. The more she expressed gratitude, the better she felt. So she kept expressing gratitude. She would say "thank you" over and over in her mind and she would express gratitude and kindness to everyone. And everything changed….

EXERCISE:

Find 100 things you can be grateful for over the next week.

HIDE-AND-STAY-SEEK

If you play hide-and-go-seek and you hide in the same spot every single time, it would be silly for you to get upset with others when they easily find you. If you don't want them to find you, you will have to hide in a new spot – otherwise, you're really just playing "hide-and-stay-seek." Hide-and-stay-seek is not very much fun to play.

Sometimes you might feel like others know what to do to push your buttons. You might think, "They know how to get to me!" But the only reason that they might know how to get to you is *if you respond* in the same way to them as you always have.

What about trying a new "hiding spot?"

Don't play hide-and-stay-seek anymore. The more you grow personally – the more you change and grow – the more difficult it will be for others to ever figure out how to "get at" you, let alone "push your buttons."

Find a new spot in the space of your life. Make it a peaceful place. Make it a place of self-control. Make it a place of peaceful self-talk. Make it a place where you speak in kind ways to others. Make it a place of gratitude. The more you rely on self-control, peaceful self-talk, kind speech, and gratitude, the more peace you will find. Once you find it, practice keeping it. The more you practice peace, the faster you will attain having it all the time. Peace doesn't have to remain hidden from you anymore.

EXERCISE:

What can people do to push your buttons?

_____

_____

_____

_____

What is the benefit you get for allowing others to have control over your "buttons"? (For example, when you allow others to have control over your mind, you might convince yourself that you're not responsible for what you do… etc.)

_____

_____

_____

_____

What is the benefit to you for taking complete control of your mind and no longer giving others the power to "push your buttons"?

_____

_____

_____

_____

What can you do to change your buttons so that people can no longer have the power to push them?

_____

_____

_____

_____

None of us want to be seen as a puppet, but the reality is that every time you allow others to "push your buttons," you are also allowing them to pull your strings and move you about like a puppet. The most effective way to stop allowing others to make you their puppet is to take complete control of your life - and only **you** have the power to do that.

"You are not a puppet - unless you allow yourself to be."

- Dr. Christian Conte

28

PEACEFUL WORDS, PEACEFUL MIND

Remember that although the outside world doesn't determine what goes on in your inner world, the reality is that what you surround yourself with impacts you. The more you surround yourself with peaceful images and sayings, the more you fill your mind with the type of peace that you want to actually be in your mind. The following page is an example of a type of poster that you can put up on your wall to remind you of all the positive, healthy words that can be helpful to replay over and again in your mind.

EXERCISE:

Consider hanging up the following page (with the kind of words that would be healthy for you to remember to keep in the front of your mind) somewhere you can see it regularly; or maybe consider making your own poster of positive, loving, and peaceful words. Having zero thoughts is very difficult (if not impossible) to do since your mind will inevitably have some thoughts running through it. It's wise to do your best to repeat the kinds of words and phrases in your mind that will most likely lead to a sense of peace.

Loving-kindness

Compassion

Light

Goodness

Gratitude

Peace

Love

Kind-heartedness

Gentleness

Graciousness

Calm

Generosity

Forgiveness

29

WHAT LEADS TO WHAT

When you jump up in the air, you come back down. When you run, you move faster than when you walk. When you eat enough food, you get full. When you fall asleep, you are not awake. When you swim in water, you get wet. Whatever you do leads to a consequence - and sometimes those consequences are pretty obvious, and others times not so much. But sometimes, the consequences of our thoughts and actions are obvious, but we just don't take the time to think about them very much. In this exercise, take some time to think about the obvious consequences of your thoughts and actions.

What I feel good doing is: _____

What I feel bad doing is: _____

When I feel good, my thoughts are centered on: _____

What I feel bad, my thoughts are centered on: _____

What makes me feel good about myself is doing:_____

What I do that hurts me is: _____

When I think _____ I end up feeling like _____

When I feel like _____ I start to think _____

When I pull myself out of a tough time, these are the kind of thoughts that I think:

_____

When I pull myself out of a tough time, these are the kinds of behaviors that I do:

_____

When I exercise regularly, I feel: _____

When I do: _____ every day, I feel _____

When I forget to: _____, I start to feel bad mentally.

When I forget to: _____, I start to feel bad physically.

When I do: _____, I start to feel bad spiritually.

When I talk about others and gossip, I feel: _____ about myself.

When I rise above negativity, I feel: _____ about myself.

When I take the time to: _____ I feel the best about myself.

My thoughts and feelings are connected. My feelings and thoughts are connected. What I think drives what I feel. What I feel impacts what I think. The more aware I can be of my thoughts, the more in control of my feelings I can be. The more I can understand the connection between my thoughts and feelings, the more I can change my thoughts to focus on what I want: Peace.

"The more you know what leads to what, the better chance you have to follow the path that takes you to where you actually want to go."

- Dr. Christian Conte

30

EMOTIONAL CONTROL

The term "**emotion-regulation**" refers to **your ability to control how you feel**.

"It's not the end of the world," said many peaceful people.

Uncomfortable feelings can suck; but the reality is that they are inevitable. We will all feel uncomfortable feelings from time to time. That is why increasing your ability to tolerate uncomfortable feelings is important. Remember, we all master what we practice, so the more you practice tolerating uncomfortable situations, the better you get at it. The more upset/angry you get over a situation, the less of a chance you have to see what might really be going on.

The more overly critical you are about a situation, the less time you have to "work the problem" and focus on solutions. When a problem happens, you basically have two choices: You can either start complaining about how whatever happened "shouldn't have happened," or you can start working on a solution. The choice is yours. How you focus your energy is entirely up to you. You master what you practice, and the more you practice taking deep breaths, stepping back, seeing the bigger picture, and taking time to control your thoughts by saying things like, "I'm okay," and "I can handle this," and "It's not the end of the world," the better you will get at relying on those types of thoughts when it comes time to draw on them in tougher, uncomfortable situations.

Questions

1. Who is in control of your thoughts? _____

Now list some of the people you have allowed to be in control of your thoughts:

_____

_____

_____

2. Can you change the past?_____

If your answer is "no," then describe what makes you focus so much on the past:

_____

_____

_____

3. Can you stop others from saying and doing things that you don't want them to say and do (if your answer is "no," then describe what makes you try to control others' speech and behaviors)?

_____

_____

_____

_____

4. What can you control?

_____

_____

5. When you spend time complaining rather than working the problem, what does it do for you?

_____

_____

_____

_____

6. What are advantages of working the problem instead of complaining?

_____

_____

_____

_____

7. How can people experience more peaceful thoughts?

_____

_____

_____

_____

8. What steps can you take to be more in control of your thoughts?

_____

_____

_____

_____

9. In the space below, write a brief story about a woman who found her strength and learned how to regulate (control) her emotions:

_____

_____

_____

_____

_____

_____

_____

_____

_____

_____

_____

_____

_____

_____

_____

_____

"Regulating your emotions takes effort, but the result is worth your effort."

- Dr. Christian Conte

31

POSITIVE THINKING

It can be tough to "think positive" when you're going through a tough moment; but the reality is that the more you focus on the strengths you have, the better you feel. The fact is, though: **You have survived every single difficult moment of your life.** You are strong enough to get through anything you are facing now, and everything you ever will face in the future.

"I can overcome anything."

My favorite thing about me is: _____.

My best quality is: _____.

What I'm most proud of myself for doing in my life is:

_____.

The strongest part about me is: _____.

The best thing I ever made was: _____.

The most caring thing I've ever done for someone was:

_____.

The most I ever helped someone out when they least expected it was:

_____.

One of the nicest things I ever did for someone that hardly anyone knows I did was:

_____

The biggest obstacle I was ever able to overcome was:

_____.

The biggest accomplishment of my life is:_____.

My favorite thing to laugh about is: _____.

The most spiritual experience I ever had was:

_____.

The kindest thing I ever did for a stranger was: _____.

The best emotional experience of my life was:

_____.

What calms my mind the most is:_____.

The best thing I ever did when I was a little kid was_____.

The most kind act I ever did as a teenager was_____.

The most thoughtful thing anyone ever did for me was:

_____.

The funniest thing I ever did _____.

The most peaceful I ever felt was _____.

The happiest I ever was, was_____.

The smartest thing I ever did was _____.

The most in control of myself I ever was, was _____.

The best way that I balance my emotions is_____.

The silliest thing I ever did with friends was:

_____.

The most peaceful place in the world is: _____.

What I'm most excited about sharing with the world is:_____.

My favorite talent that I have is:_____.

The best friendship quality I have is:_____.

The best part about me in relationships is:_____.

What I feel most proud about myself for doing is: _____.

What I feel most proud about myself for saying is:_____.

The best thing I could teach others to help them feel more positive

is:_____.

REPEAT DAILY:

I am strong.

    I am smart.   I am funny.

I am beautiful.   I am loving.   I am kind.

    I am grateful.   I am forgiving.   I am compassionate.

I am happy.   I am honest.   I am optimistic.

    I am thoughtful.   I am considerate.

I am aware.   I am trustworthy.

    I am good.

I am….

I am_____.

I am_____.

I am_____.

I am_____.

I am_____.

I am_____.

I am_____.

"You are an incredible miracle of life. You have incredible potential to impact more people than you can see. The past is gone - and the only thing that matters now is what you do from this moment forward."

\- Dr. Christian Conte

32

WATCHING MYSELF

The more you can observe yourself, the more you can see what others see. When you step back and look inward, you will be able to fully understand that people only see your actions, not your intentions. Others only see what you do, they cannot see what you think. The more you watch yourself, the more you'll see yourself.

Right now I feel: _____.

From the outside, when I am angry, this is what I look like:

_____.

When I am sad, this is what I look like to others:

_____.

When I am anxious, this is what I look like to others:

_____.

When I am in a good space mentally, this is what I look like to others:

_____.

This is what I can do to get myself in a good place mentally:

_____

This is how others experience me when I am complaining: _____

_____

This is how others experience me when I am angry:_____

_____

This is how others experience me when I gossip:_____

_____

This is how others experience me when I have to be "right":_____

_____

This is how others experience me when I am negative:_____

_____

This is how others experience me when I act helpless:_____

_____

If I had to put an image to my feelings, it would be:_____

When others are around me, they feel:_____

When others walk away from me, they think:_____

The more you can see yourself as accurately as others can see you, the better chance you have to change the things you need to change to live your best possible life. Take time to step back and observe yourself as often as you can. See yourself through others' eyes and watch the difference in not only the way you interact with others, but also with how others interact with you.

Professional Tip: When professional counselors have a challenging interaction with their clients, the first thing they do is evaluate the role they played in that interaction. Instead of looking at what their client did "wrong," they look at what they (themselves) might have done to trigger such behavior in their client. By focusing on the role they play in the interaction, they have a better chance at evaluating their clients accurately, and they also have a better chance at being more effective with future clients. Professional counselors spend their whole career trying to understand what impact their words and actions have on others, which is why professional counselors are most effective when they understand their own role in every interaction they have. You don't need a degree in counseling, psychology, or social work to work really hard at constantly trying to understand how others perceive you. The more you understand how others perceive you, the better you get at learning how to communicate well.

"My peace is a gift of my own creation."
– Dr. Christian Conte

33

COMPLICATED

We are all more complicated than what others see. Being able to express yourself completely is difficult; but the only way others will ever know even a little bit of what's going on inside of you is if you at least try to share with them what you can.

I feel: _____.

I think: _____.

I want: _____.

I believe: _____.

I expect: _____.

I try to: _____.

I can't: _____.

I won't: _____.

I should: _____.

I will: _____.

We have a tendency to think that we are really deep and mysterious, but others are shallow and predictable. Unfortunately, others see us the exact same way. The truth is that we are all deep and mysterious in ways, but also shallow and predictable in other ways. In short, we are complicated beings.

The more you can figure out what's going on with you mentally, physically, and spiritually, the more accurately you can communicate that to others. Also, the more you can see accurately what is going on inside of you, the more understanding you'll be of others who are also equally complicated.

Here are examples of statements that directly convey to others what's going on with you:

(Maybe none of these statements are statements you feel like you would actually say. Maybe the way they're worded sounds so ridiculous that they make you laugh. On the other hand, maybe one or two of them fits with you, and you could start using them right away. The point isn't to give you direct statements that you *have* to start saying, the point is to see that in each case, ***the goal is to communicate clearly that you are experiencing physical or psychological discomfort, and you are aware that your mind always wants to match your body.*** The more aware you are that your mind wants to match your body, the fewer stories you will feel like you need to create to make sense of it all.)

"I stopped taking medicine, and I know that anytime a person changes medicine, it can have an impact on her. I feel really agitated/irritable right now, but I know it's because I just changed/stopped taking medicine. I know this feeling is temporary, so even though it's uncomfortable, I know it will pass."

"I feel really anxious right now, and I'm aware that my brain is trying to create a story to match it."

"I feel really sad right now, and I don't feel like I have a reason to be sad, so I'm thinking that something might be off chemically for me right now. I'd like to find out what it is."

"I'm sorry, but I feel very anxious right now, and I don't want or need you to fix it; but I just want you to know that if I seem off, it's because I'm going through a lot right now."

"Hey, I can tell that I feel chemically off right now, so please don't take anything personally if I come across as agitated or irritable in any way. I just honestly feel agitated right now."

"If I seem distracted right now, it's because I honestly just don't feel well physically right now. Please don't take anything I say personally because I know that what's going on with me has nothing to do with you (even though my brain keeps insisting that you're to blame…)."

"I can tell I am probably coming across as short right now. I feel agitated, and I'm not sure what it might be."

"I drank way too much caffeine today, so if I come across as anxious, please know that's why."

"I drank a lot of caffeine yesterday, and I haven't had any yet today, so if I seem really irritable, it's because my body just feels irritable from not having caffeine right now."

"My body feels so agitated right now, and I'm not sure why I feel so agitated, but I realize that it's physical, so I want to make sure I don't allow myself to make up an angry story right now."

"I can tell that I feel anxious right now, and I know that lashing out in anger would probably make me feel better, but I know I'd probably regret whatever I'd say or do out of anger, so I'm going to just take some time to sit with this emotion - especially because I know it will eventually pass."

"I'm sorry ahead of time for how I'm coming across. I promise it's not you, it's what's going on with me. I just feel so agitated/irritable inside right now that I want to find something to be angry at…."

"I have a lot going on right now, so I don't want to make any big decisions when I feel this badly physically."

"I changed medicine recently, and I know doing that can really impact how I feel, so I want to be mindful that I might be feeling off a little for the next couple days."

"I want you to know that I didn't sleep well last night, and I know that when I don't sleep well, I tend to be more irritable - so I just want to apologize ahead of time for how I might come across right now."

"You know, I don't really know what's going on with me right now, but I know that I don't want to make up a story to make it feel worse, so I'm just going to sit with how I feel for a little bit. I know that however I'm feeling will eventually change…."

In each of the instances above, the goal is to state what's going on with you, and then do your best to not go with the story your mind creates in a race to match your body. Your mind will want to match your body, but with practice, you can learn to master sitting with tough emotions until they pass without saying or doing anything that you regret along the way. All emotions are temporary, so do your best to learn how to communicate what's going on with you as clearly as possible.

34

THE RABBIT WHO TOOK EVERYTHING PERSONALLY

A rabbit went hopping through the woods, and she talked to every animal she encountered. Now this rabbit didn't feel very good about herself. She struggled with her self-esteem. She often felt hurt inside. And because she felt hurt, she tended to take things personally.

She walked up to a squirrel who was eating an acorn, and the rabbit asked, "Why would you do that to me?" The squirrel was surprised at such a silly question, so he asked her in return, "What do you mean *'do this to me'*? I'm just eating!" But the rabbit thought the squirrel was lying, and she took what he was doing personally.

The rabbit then bounced up to a bear and the bear, was scratching her back on a tree, and the rabbit asked the bear, "Why would you do that to me?" And the bear was taken back, and asked, "How am I doing this to you? I'm just scratching my itchy back." But the rabbit took it personally.

The rabbit ran around and around and did the same thing to all the animals she encountered. Whomever she met, whatever they were doing, time and again, she took what other animals did personally – even though none of it was directed toward her.

Because rabbit didn't feel good about herself inside, she really convinced herself that what other animals did was aimed at her, but here's the thing: It wasn't. What the other animals did, they did because they were going to do regardless of meeting the rabbit.

One day the rabbit walked up to an old and wise turtle, and when she saw him put his head back in his shell, she asked him, "Why would you do that to me?" But the turtle wasn't like the other animals, and instead of looking at her strangely or asking her a question in return, he taught her something. He taught her how to catch herself anytime she started to take something personally that wasn't personal. And it took awhile. It took awhile for her to learn how to avoid taking things personally, but eventually, she learned how to stop doing it.

The lessons the rabbit learned that helped her not take everything personally were these:

- None of us gets everything we want in life.

- Everyone struggles in life, and just the way the rabbit has unintentionally lashed out at others at times in her life (and it wasn't personal toward others), she realized that others also unintentionally say and do things that they don't always mean, either.

- People only give others what is inside of them – so if they are peaceful inside, they give peace; if they feel upset inside, they give anxiety, anger and pain…. But none of it is personal.

The rabbit also learned that *we master what we practice*, and just the way she got very good at taking things personally (because that's what she used to practice) – with practice and over time, she eventually became very good at not taking things personally anymore – and she was much, much happier.

1. Describe a time when you took something personally that later on you found out wasn't personal toward you at all:

_____

_____

_____

_____

2. What kinds of things can you do to remind yourself that what others do isn't personal toward you?

_____

_____

_____

_____

The more you take other people's words and actions personally, the more upset you will be. The more you can recognize that people only ever hurt others from a place of pain themselves, the more peace you will find.

"As difficult as it might be to realize, the reality is that people have to be very self-centered to believe that others' behavior is personal toward them."

- Dr. Christian Conte

35

TRUTHS

It's wise to fill your mind with the kind of thoughts that you want to be in your mind.

No one controls your destiny but you.

Your present situation is a result of your past choices; your future situation will be a result of what you choose from this moment forward.

Your mind is infinitely stronger than you realize. Your body is tremendously more capable than you know. When you believe in yourself and your abilities, you become more capable of achieving anything you pursue.

There is a beginning, middle, and end to every emotional situation. Be mindful not to make a decision in the beginning or middle of a tough emotion that leaves you with a result you don't want long after that tough emotion passes.

You are stronger than you think. You can do this.

You have the ability to fight the urge to be impulsive. You have the ability to fight for yourself. You are worth it.

You have survived every single tough experience from your past.

You are a warrior.

You are the hero in the adventure story of your life.

EXERCISE:

Write your own truths below. Write truths that you have learned from your experience in life:

_____

_____

_____

_____

_____

_____

_____

_____

_____

_____

_____

_____

_____

_____

Your experiences in life are invaluable. When you take the time to look deeply within, you will see that you have the answers you need to guide you to where you want to go. Knowing answers and living them out are of course two very different endeavors, but the more you state your truths out loud, the more clearly you can live them out.

36

HOW TO HANDLE AGITATION AND IRRITABILITY

Everyone feels agitated and irritable from time to time. You will feel agitated and irritable sometimes. There are so many factors that contribute to feeling agitated, but some of the factors include:

- Change in medicine

- Hormones

- Hunger

- Lack of sleep

- Stress

- Anxiety

- Depression

When you feel agitated and irritable, the chances are that you will magnify and personalize outside events much more so than you would if your body felt good. There is also a significantly better chance that you will lash out at others and blame them for how you're feeling, when the real source of you feeling the way you do is agitation and irritability.

So what can you do?

When you feel agitated or irritable, you can:

- Lash out at others and make your situation worse

- Make a "mountain out of the mole hills" in front of you, and make your situation worse

- Use extreme language like "always," and "never," and "can't stand it!" and make your situation worse

Or you can:

- Sit with your feelings and not lash out impulsively

- Work on increasing your mindfulness about how you feel, the types of things you say to yourself, and the way your environment impacts you

- Tell yourself peaceful sayings like, "I'm okay," and "I'm safe," and "I can handle this…."

1. Describe an experience where you felt irritable or agitated and lashed out at others, when really you were just hurting inside:

_____

_____

_____

_____

2. If you could go back in time and handle that situation more effectively, what could you have done differently?

_____

_____

_____

_____

3. Describe a time when you felt agitated or irritable but chose to NOT lash out at others:

_____

_____

_____

_____

4. What was it that you were able to do to keep yourself from taking your irritability or agitation out on others?

_____

_____

_____

_____

As you have seen over and over in this workbook, there is a beginning, middle and end to every emotional situation, and that is especially true for when you feel agitated or irritable. The feelings of agitation and irritability eventually pass, but the actions you do and the words you say when you feel agitated and irritable cannot be taken back. Be mindful to sit with your emotions rather than impulsively react to them. Your emotions will pass. Irritability and agitation will pass, what you say and do while you feel that way cannot be "taken back," however. **Do your best not to be reactive the next time you feel agitated or irritable**.

Agitation and irritability are uncomfortable, but they are not insurmountable. In other words, as difficult as it is to experience uncomfortable situations, they are not impossible to overcome. The more you can be aware of how you feel, the less pressure you put on yourself to solve your feelings, and the easier it is to get through them. You are not your emotions. Your emotions do not result in consequences; the actions you do based on how you feel are what result in consequences.

"Emotions are temporary. Actions last forever. The wise understand the difference."

- Dr. Christian Conte

37

MAGNIFY AND PERSONALIZE

When we're suffering on the inside, we have a tendency to do two things: **Magnify** and **personalize**. To magnify is to make something bigger than it needs to be. To personalize something is to take something personal that's not personal.

There are situations that we make bigger than they are, and there are things that we take personally that simply aren't personal.

Magnifying:

We magnify events with the language we use to describe them. For example, if someone says something to you, and you describe what they say with adjectives like, "She keeps coming at me with…" or "He keeps throwing in my face that…" those are examples of magnifying a situation. If someone is "coming at you," then that literally means they are moving forward toward you. For that statement to be accurate, a person would have to be continually moving toward you and closing in on you; otherwise, saying that someone is "coming at you," is an exaggeration and an example of magnifying. Similarly, if you use a statement like, "She's throwing that in my face," that is also an example of magnifying. Again, in order for that statement to be accurate, a person would have to be literally throwing something at your face.

When you magnify a situation, you make yourself much angrier than you need to be, and it makes sense why. The more you feel like you need to physically protect yourself, the more likely you are to react angrily. The problem with magnifying is that it makes you feel unnecessarily defensive. Unless someone is continually physically coming straight toward you or literally throwing objects at your face, the reality is that you are magnifying the situation by describing it that way.

Personalizing:

Everyone struggles. There have been times in your life when you were struggling and you took it out on others, even though those others didn't deserve you doing that. In those moments, it would have benefitted others to not take the pain you were feeling personally. In the same way, it's important for you to not take other people's pain personally. Displacement occurs when you "displace" (or put) anger or pain from one area of your life onto a completely different area. So, if you are angry or hurt by one person, but you take it out on someone else, then you are displacing your feelings. Everyone displaces from time to time.

When others lash out at you, it's important to step back and recognize that it is highly likely that their pain is not personal toward you, even if it seems or feels like it is. We can only ever give others what is inside of us, and others can only ever give us what is inside of them. In other words, if others are hurting inside, they might give us that hurt or take that hurt out on us (unfairly), and it's important to understand that their pain is not personal to us. Specifically, other people's pain is not personal toward you.

The fact that you have magnified and personalized situations in your life is completely normal. All of us have done that from time to time. The goal is to become aware of when you are magnifying or personalizing, because the more aware you are of when you do it, the better chance you have at not doing it.

1. Give an example of a time when you magnified a situation that didn't need to be magnified:

_____

_____

_____

_____

2. What types of words or phrases did you use to make that situation bigger than it needed to be?

_____

_____

_____

_____

3. Give an example of a time when you took other people's pain personally:

_____

_____

_____

_____

4. What can you do differently to avoid taking other people's pain personally in the future?

_____

_____

_____

_____

You do not need to make things bigger than they are. It's okay to tell people that you are hurting more than what they see. Like everyone else on the planet, your mind is vastly deeper than you can show others. There is no measurable way to describe the pain you're feeling, and sometimes when you're hurting you will want so badly for others to understand what you're going through that you will take great effort to describe (and sometimes exaggerate) what you are feeling inside. This is magnification.

Just the way you have unintentionally hurt others, others have unintentionally hurt you. When you find yourself convinced that others intentionally hurt you, be mindful that others that you have hurt in the past probably think the same thing about you. The truth is likely different, though. The reality is that we all hurt each other from a place of pain. It's wise not to personalize the pain that others have. It's wise to avoid taking things personally that simply aren't personal.

We have a tendency to minimize the harm we cause others and maximize the harm others cause us. The more you can be aware that you mind will try to convince you to downplay the hurt you cause others and exaggerate the pain others cause you, the more you will be able to gain a realistic picture of what really happened. The more you accept full responsibility for your actions, the more quickly you learn how to avoid magnifying or personalizing what doesn't need to be magnified or personalized.

38

MY PERSONAL STRENGTH JOURNAL ENTRY

By_____

MESSAGE TO MYSELF: I've gone through a lot in my life. I've had good times and tough times, but the one truth is that I have survived every single difficult experience I've ever had. I'm strong, and I have a lot to offer the world. I have the ability to teach others how to get through even the toughest experiences, because I can lead by example.

I find that the more I focus on taking care of myself, the better things are for me. I know, too, that the more I focus on the things I *can* do – and the things that I actually have control over – the better I feel. At the end of the day, I have learned time and again, when I use the wisdom I have gained throughout my life, I handle even the toughest times more effectively.

I recognize that people only see what I do, and they cannot see in my mind; but I can see in my mind. I know that sometimes a lot goes on in my mind that I almost wish others could see. Journaling is a great way to get some of my inner thoughts down on paper so I can see them. Journaling helps me express myself. I have learned how to navigate through my inner world. I have learned how to express my thoughts – to say what's going on inside of me. I know others can only see my actions and hear what I say (not what I "meant to say" or "didn't mean to say"); I know that, just the way I only see other people's actions, other people only ever see my actions. In journaling, I help myself get a clearer picture of what is going on in my mind, and *that* ultimately helps me express myself more clearly to others – that way, when they do see my actions, they see me doing my best actions.

Everything that has happened in my life has led me to this moment. Everything I've gone through has taught me. I have learned a lot about myself. I know I can write anything in this journal, but I like the idea of journaling about the successes I've had. I like the idea of journaling about the wisdom I've gained, and the ways I actually practice using the wisdom I have. I like highlighting my strengths, because I alone know the full extent of everything I've gone through and how I use my strength all the time. I alone know the wisdom that I can share with the world.

I know I have a purpose. I know my purpose is bigger than me. I know I'm strong. I know I'm capable. I know I can get through any difficult time I ever encounter. I believe in me. I believe in my potential, and I believe in who I am right now. I know that I am my own best coach, and this journal entry is a great reflection of that. These are the most incredible things about me - and these are the things I want to remind myself of when times get hard in the future:

_____

_____

_____

_____

_____

_____

_____

_____

_____

_____

_____

_____

_____

_____

_____

_____

_____

_____

_____

_____

Even though sometimes it's hard for me to acknowledge the good things about me (and I know it's tough for me to take a compliment), the reality is that:

I am so proud of myself because:

_____

_____

_____

_____

What I like best about myself is:

_____

_____

_____

_____

The good message I want to give the world is:

_____

_____

_____

_____

The most peaceful thoughts I tend to have are:

_____

_____

_____

_____

The way I like to show others my most compassionate energy is:

_____

_____

_____

_____

I know others only see my actions, not my intentions, so the best way for others to *see* the good changes I'm making is:

_____

_____

_____

_____

The best way for me to handle tough emotions is:

_____

_____

_____

_____

What I've learned about myself through the years is:

_____

_____

_____

_____

The healthiest habits for me to do every day to take care of my body, mind and spirit are:

Body:

_____

_____

_____

_____

Mind:

_____

_____

_____

_____

Spirit:

_____

_____

_____

_____

The most peaceful thoughts that are great for me to repeat to myself over and over as often as possible are:

_____

_____

_____

_____

"Every experience I've ever had has led me to having the wisdom I now have."

39

THE LESSONS LITTLE GRASSHOPPER LEARNED

A little grasshopper wanted to go with the older grasshoppers to the pond. She asked her mother if she could go, and her mother said, "No," because her mother was worried about her little grasshopper.

The little grasshopper started screaming and crying and throwing herself on the ground. She started calling her mother names and pounding the ground, but her mother just looked at the little grasshopper with confusion. Her mother smiled, took a deep, loving breath, and said in a calm, compassionate voice, "Why would you think that I would allow you to get what you want if you act like that?"

The little grasshopper didn't have a logical answer, so she didn't say anything in reply.

Her mother then said, "We teach others how to treat us. We also teach others about us with everything we say and do. Right now, you are teaching me that you will say and do anything to try to get what you want, and you are also teaching me how to treat you. I will never give in when you act like that. You will never get anything you want if you act like that. If you want something from me, you will need to learn to treat me in the same loving-kind way that I am treating you right now. You will need to learn to speak with kindness and patience and calmness and love."

Her mother continued, "And you will also need to learn that you will not get everything you ask for in life. So there is a big difference between asking for something (and truly asking – meaning you are prepared for whatever the answer might be), and demanding something. You will not get many things in life if you are mean and angry and demanding. And even though you will not get everything you want in life anyway, you will get many more things that you want when you learn to ask with kindness and compassion than you will ever get by screaming out and yelling and being mean or demanding."

When her mother finished speaking, the little grasshopper felt embarrassed by her behavior. She started to hang her head and feel bad about herself. Maybe even deep down this little grasshopper thought if she now felt bad enough – maybe her mother would feel sorry for her feeling so bad – and maybe her mother would give in to what she wanted. But her mother then surprised her with another lesson:

Her mother then said, "I do not want you to feel shame; I want you to learn the lesson." She continued, "Trying to make yourself the victim now, and acting like a poor helpless victim because I corrected you will not lead to you getting what you want, either. Look, little grasshopper, and listen to this lesson: The past is gone and we cannot ever get even one single second of it back, but what we can do is learn from the past and be better from this moment forward. You are not 'bad' or 'terrible,' you just tried to get what you wanted by doing something that didn't work (i.e., screaming and yelling and being mean). My job is to teach you in life. Your job is to learn as many lessons as you can. The faster you learn, the more peace you will have."

The lessons her mother taught her that day were:

- You are not likely to get what you want by yelling and screaming and being mean to the person you want something from, because it is better to be kind and compassionate and patient than it is to be angry and mean

- With everything you say and do, you are teaching people how to treat you

- Once you mess up and are called on it, instead of "playing the victim" and feeling sorry for yourself, it is better to simply learn from your mistakes

The little grasshopper was glad her mother taught her these lessons. She realized in that moment that the lessons her mother just taught her was infinitely better than being allowed to go to the pond that day.

From that moment forward, the little grasshopper was always mindful about the way she asked for things. She knew she wouldn't get everything she wanted in life, but she especially knew that she only ever had a much worse chance of getting anything as long as she was mean and hurtful and demanding. On that day, with that lesson (and the other lessons her mother taught her), the little grasshopper became extremely wise.

"You are not asked to be perfect in this life. You are only ever asked to give the best you can with what you have in every moment."

"You will get farther with kindness and compassion and patience, than you will ever get with anger and mean comments and demands."

1. In what ways have you acted in the past like the little grasshopper:

_____

_____

_____

_____

2. How do you respond to others when they scream and yell and demand that you get them things?

_____

_____

_____

_____

3. Give an example of a time when you did the "poor me" routine to try to get out of being in trouble:

_____

_____

_____

_____

4. Give an example of a time when you owned complete responsibility for your behaviors and just learned from them:

_____

_____

_____

_____

40

A CLEAR PATH

You have the potential to achieve any goal that you want to achieve. Every goal takes effort. If you start at the end of every goal and work backwards, you can see the clear path to your goal. The more clear your goals are, the more clear the path to those goals are. For example, if what you truly want in life is peace or to regulate your emotions regardless of what's going on around you, then the path to work on that is clear: Every day pay attention to your thoughts; every day work on putting effort into not acting on your impulses. The more you practice, the better you get.

1. What goals do you really, truly want to achieve in life?

_____

_____

_____

_____

2. What are you honestly doing every single day/week/month to work toward those goals?

_____

_____

_____

_____

3. How can you do more of what will actually get you what you want?

_____

_____

_____

_____

4. What stops you from doing what you need to do to get what you want?

_____

_____

_____

_____

5. What can you reasonably do to overcome any obstacles that get in the way of you achieving your goals?

_____

_____

_____

_____

In the space below, draw a quick sketch of what your path to peace will look like from this moment forward:

41

WALKING ON RICE PAPER

There are legends of great martial artists who have mastered being able to walk on rice paper without making any marks on it, let alone ripping it. Rice paper is very thin, and the only way to walk on thin paper without ripping it is to do so carefully, patiently, and with intention to walk softly. Anyone who sets out to walk across rice paper without ripping it has to do so with a sense of quiet peacefulness: The type of quiet peacefulness you might expect to see in a Zen master.

If you were to walk on rice paper and then lash out impulsively or act rashly, you would rip it. There is way you can practice "walking on rice paper" in your life; and doing so might just bring you an incredible amount of peace. The more you can work on quieting your mind, the easier it will be to walk as though you are on rice paper all the time.

Why in the world would I want to "walk on rice paper" in my life?

The benefit to "walking on rice paper" is this: The more you are mindful about the way you walk, the more present you will be. Literally walking on rice paper isn't always possible of course, but pretending as though there is rice paper underneath your feet can change the way you visualize going about your life.

How would I go about practicing "walking on rice paper" in my life?

To master "walking on rice paper," be mindful to do the following:

- Bring a sense of stillness to your body
- Practice breathing slowly and intentionally
- Focus on quieting your body and moving with purpose
- Focus on being present in the moment
- Focus on leading with compassion
- Focus on smiling on the inside
- Focus on feeling gratitude
- Focus on peace

Ways to rip the rice paper:

- Overreact to situations

- Make mountains out of mole hills

- Use extreme words such as "always" and "never" or "terrible" and "awful" or "can't stand it" and "can't take it" to describe situations

- Be impulsive

- Speak with a loud voice

- Demand that others say and do whatever you want

Ways to master "walking on rice paper:"

- Be mindful of your breath

- Be mindful of your tone

- Be mindful of your body

- Be mindful of your thoughts

- Be mindful of the way you speak

- Be mindful of your strength and your ability to make it through tough emotional situations without it being "the end of the world"

- Be mindful that your goal in life is to control the only person over whom you actually have control: You

- Be mindful to let go of all the things over which you have no control

1. Here are two examples of situations where I see now that I overreacted at the time:

_____

_____

_____

_____

2. Here are two ways that I have shown anger unnecessarily to others:

_____

_____

_____

_____

3. Here are two things that I will keep in mind from this moment forward so that I can become better at walking on the rice paper of life:

_____

_____

_____

_____

Walk on Rice Paper, Not Eggshells

There is a big difference between "walking on eggshells" and "walking on rice paper." Both of these phrases are metaphors, but "walking on eggshells" means that you are always worried about making someone else angry; whereas "walking on rice paper," is about intentionally walking peacefully in your life.

"You alone are in control of your breath.
You alone are in control of your thoughts."

- Dr. Christian Conte

KEEPING MY CONTROL

Other people sometimes struggle just as you sometimes struggle. To be in control of your own life is to accept that others are who they are, and you cannot change others, only yourself. In every interaction, instead of saying things like, "I can't believe she said_____!" or "I can't believe he did_____!" – take the time to believe it. Believe that people will sometimes say and do things that you don't want them to say and do. Believe that people will be who they've shown you they are. When you take a moment to step back and "believe it," it will help you be more prepared to accept it.

Yes, people will say and do things that you don't want them to, but it's not personal toward you – and you overreacting only hurts the situation (and oftentimes, yourself). You can handle a lot more than you often tell yourself that you can. The more you tell yourself things like, "I can handle this," and "It's not the end of the world, the more control you have over your thoughts and feelings. And the more you can control your thoughts and feelings, the more peace you invite into your life.

In life, you might regret a lot of things, but you will never regret being compassionate and forgiving. You will never regret being in control of your thoughts and emotions. And more than anything, you will never regret feeling peace.

- Practice being in control of your thoughts by saying things like:

"I'm okay."

"I can handle this."

"It's not the end of the world."

The fact is: You ARE okay. You CAN handle this. And no matter what you're experiencing, it's NOT the end of the world.

"Everything changes, including every difficult feeling you ever have."

- Dr. Christian Conte

THE MIRACULOUS MORNING

The goddess of the sea had weathered a terrible storm. The storm lasted for weeks, and there was darkness everywhere. The goddess of the sea, as incredible as she was, found herself lost in this great storm…. But she was a warrior. She was powerful and strong, and even though this storm was strong, the truth was: She was stronger.

The goddess of the sea outlasted the storm, and then something miraculous happened the following morning: The sun came out! The sky was beautiful and there was a great calm all throughout the waters. There was clarity everywhere. The goddess of the sea felt a great calmness all throughout her body, mind, and spirit - and peace begin to pour through her and flow through any wounds that the storm created.

As peace moved throughout ocean, the goddess of the sea returned to her true nature; her true form. She was awake again. This time she was awake for good. The goddess of the sea had weathered the great storm, and she awakened to a sense of peace that now filled her mind and soul entirely.

It was a beautiful feeling: She was herself again.

EXERCISE:

Imagine that you woke up tomorrow morning and felt complete inner peace. Think about what your thoughts would look like. Think about what you would do differently. Once you have a good idea of what your thoughts would look like and what you would do if you felt complete peace, consider practicing the things you know you would think and do in a state of inner peace.

INNER TORNADOS

We all experience inner tornados from time to time. Inner tornados occur when our thoughts start spinning really fast, usually about negative things. There are lots of causes of inner tornados, but none of those causes occur from the outside. The real cause of inner tornados are things that go on inside of us. Sometimes when we feel off physically, our thoughts start to match the storm we have inside.

There are two important lessons to understand about inner tornados:

1. When you are experiencing an inner tornado, try your best to avoid attributing your tornado to outside events or people. In other words, recognize that the inner tornado is happening within – because the sooner you realize that it is happening from within, the sooner you can realize that you also have the ability to handle the storm on the inside as well.

2. When others are experiencing an inner tornado, nothing they say and do is personal toward you – so it's extremely important not to engage in arguments with them or "feed the storm."

Strategies for handling your inner tornados:

- Be mindful of your self-talk
- Try to be an observer of what's going on inside you without reacting to it
- Be as accurate with your language as you can
- Avoid using extreme adjectives like "always," and "never"

Strategies for handling being around other people's inner tornados:

- Do not engage in arguments with them
- Do not take anything they say personally
- Understand that they are struggling, and show them compassion
- Know that their inner tornado will eventually pass, just as your own inner tornados have passed

Be easy on yourself when you're struggling.
Be easy on others when they're struggling.
Give your best to others.
Give your best to yourself

EXERCISE:

Describe the most recent "inner tornado" you felt:

_____

_____

_____

_____

What were all the contributing factors to that inner tornado?

_____

_____

_____

_____

Which factors within your control could you have handled more effectively?

_____

_____

_____

_____

What will you do differently the next time you experience an inner tornado?

_____

_____

_____

_____

"Like the weather, your emotions will constantly change."

\- Dr. Christian Conte

45

IT JUST HAPPENED!

Whatever happened is in the past. It doesn't matter if it happened 10,000 years ago or 5 seconds ago, if it "happened," it's in the past. In life, we are always faced with the choice of what to do in this moment. We are not able to do anything about the past, but we are able to do many things about the present. Whatever happened has happened, whether it happened long ago or just now. The question is: What will you do right now?

Life is tough and things don't always go our way, but we are the owner and operator of our thoughts, so we alone can create how we handle this moment right now, regardless of what happened in the previous moment or in moments long ago. The past is gone. The present is now. So again, the question is: What will you do right now?

You get to re-start your entire life from this moment forward. And every new moment is a new opportunity to start over. Focus on this moment. Focus on right here and right now, and focus on controlling the only thing over which you have complete control: What you can do right now.

Everything that you have ever done in the past has contributed to where you are in this moment. Everything you do from this moment forward will impact where you'll be in the future. Regardless of what others do, you are only ever in control of you. And you are only in control of what you do in this moment right here, right now.

To bring your mind to the present moment and help yourself make good decisions for your future self, ask yourself:

- What can I do right now?

- How will what I do right now impact me in the future?

EXERCISE:

Imagine that you felt awful inside and then lashed out and yelled at someone in a way that you later regretted. Then imagine that you could *either* spend time wishing it didn't happen or spend time learning from it. Which would you focus on, and why?

_____

_____

_____

_____

If you mess up and break a rule and get a consequence, you have a choice: You can get mad that you got that consequence and lash out and get a worse consequence, or you can accept that you made a mistake, got a consequence, and just learn from the experience. As long as we're alive, we will always make mistakes, but the key is to avoid making poor decisions once we get a consequence for the mistake we made.

Give an example of a possible mistake you could make and the consequence that would follow:

_____

_____

_____

_____

Give an example of how your reaction to getting a consequence could either make things worse for you or better for you:

_____

_____

_____

_____

The past has already happened. The future is "out there" somewhere. The present moment is the only one in which you can actually do anything.

46

DAY CARE CENTER

There were 10 children at the daycare center. Every day, the children were given a snack before their nap time. The people who ran the daycare were not in control of how many snacks were brought to them to hand out. Sometimes the food company who delivered the snacks, would bring just 10 stacks. But other times, the food company had extra, and to be nice, they would bring those extra hours to the day care center.

When they brought extra snacks, there were not always enough for everyone to have extras. This stuff had to figure out who to give the extra snacks too. Sometimes, some of the children were hungrier on particular days than others. The staff would make a judgment call as to which children to give the extra snacks to. The staff did their best at trying to be mindful to spread out the extras as equally as possible, but the children (because they were so little) would get mad and yell that things weren't "fair" if they were the ones who didn't get the extras that day. One thing that the little children didn't know, however, was that the staff had information about which children actually needed more food on certain days.

Because the children were so small (it was a daycare center, after all), they could not understand the concept of fairness. For children, especially small children, they believe that to be fair everyone has to get the exact same amount of everything. Of course, as adults we know this simply isn't true. But children, especially small children, only have the ability to think in terms of black and white. As adults, we have the ability to discern the difference between someone "needing" something versus just "wanting" it.

One thing to keep in mind, especially around these extra snacks, was that the children were never alone or entitled to getting an extra snack. That staff wanted to teach the children how to be grateful if they did get something extra, rather than throw temper tantrum's believing that they are owed extra snacks. Extra snacks, you see, were always a bonus. The extra snacks never *had* to be given out to the children.

Because these were preschool children, however, they were still learning about their world. And small children tend to believe that they are owed things. Children tend to feel "entitled" until we teach them differently. The truth is, however, even adults can feel entitled from time to time. In those moments when adults act like very small children at a daycare center who cannot handle extra snacks, sometimes adults need to be reminded that the world does not owe them anything.

If you ever find yourself in a position like those preschool children (where you believe you are owed things that you are simply not owed), one of the best things you can do is remind yourself that life is a gift, and that we are all often "owed" much less than we want. The more you understand the difference between being "owed" something and getting a privilege, the more grateful you will be.

What are you entitled to have?

_____

_____

_____

_____

What is the difference between what you "want" and what you "need"?

_____

_____

_____

_____

How can you help others understand the difference between what they *want* and what they *need?*

_____

_____

_____

_____

Gratitude can transform your soul, and it can transform your relationships. The more humble and grateful you are, the more likely others will be willing to try to get you what you want - and the more patient and understanding you'll be if they are unable to do so.

47

FINDING HER GLASSES

Once there was a woman who would slide her glasses up on her head when she didn't need them. It was just comfortable for her to keep them up on her head like that, and it was easy to slide them back down over her eyes when she needed them. At night, she would take her glasses off, and put them right next to her bed. She did the same routine all the time.

One morning, she woke up and couldn't find her glasses. She looked everywhere. She started to panic at not having them, because she needed them to read (she couldn't see the words on the pages without them). The woman's anxiety around not having her glasses soon turned to anger, and then she started to accuse others of stealing them.

Her anxiety (now manifesting as anger) overwhelmed her so much, that she started screaming at others, and then started bringing up ways in which they had wronged her in the past. She said the meanest things that would come to mind. She wanted them to hurt, too, like she was hurting from having lost her glasses. She knew somehow that everyone she yelled at couldn't possibly have all taken her glasses, but she felt justified and righteous in her anger, so she kept letting her anger erupt on anyone in her path.

And then, in the middle of her screaming at someone, in the middle of accusing the person of stealing from her, she reached up and felt her glasses on her head, where they had been all along. She realized in that moment that she must have fallen asleep with the glasses on her head, and not put them down by the bed the way she normally did. In that instant, she knew she was wrong for all she said to others, but she still had so much anger flowing through her, that she couldn't allow herself to apologize just yet, so she started accusing everyone around her of laughing at her (or some other made up reason).

Eventually, she was able to calm down, and eventually she apologized, but of course, she minimized the hurt that she caused with all the awful things she said to others. She found her glasses, but she didn't find source of her difficult emotions, and because she downplayed the hurt she caused others with her anger, she didn't learn from the experience. She misplaced her glasses, yes; but she also misplaced her anger, as well.

EXERCISE:

Do your best to help the woman from the story find the source of her anger, and help her figure out what she can do the next time she experiences anger so that A., She doesn't overreact, and B., She doesn't misplace her anger.

1. What was the real source of this woman's anger (remember that we would rather feel angry than anxious)?

_____

_____

_____

_____

2. To help this woman see that she's not alone in misplacing anger, give an example of a time when you were hurtful toward others, only to find out later on that your anger was misplaced.

_____

_____

_____

_____

3. Pride got in the way of this woman's being genuine with her apologies after she found her glasses; so even when she did apologize, she downplayed the hurt that she caused. To help this woman gain insight, give an example of a time when you downplayed the hurt you caused others, only to realize later on that what you said or did really was hurtful.

_____

_____

_____

_____

4. The next time this woman experiences anxiety or anger, what can she do to handle it more effectively (remember that there is a beginning, middle and end to every emotional experience)?

_____

_____

_____

_____

5. The woman in this story who was looking for her glasses somewhere else eventually learned that she had her glasses all along. In the same way, you and I also have answers inside of us that we sometimes expect others to have. In the space below, briefly describe a current problem you are having, and then describe what you can do to solve it on your own.

_____

_____

_____

_____

_____

_____

_____

_____

_____

_____

_____

_____

_____

"The more you look to the abilities you already have inside you to solve things, the more you see that you are capable of solving any emotional struggle that you ever encounter."

-Dr. Christian Conte

LEARNING TO PAUSE

We master what we practice. If we practice being impulsive, we become very good at being impulsive. If we practice pausing before we impulsively lash out, we become very good at that, too. At some point in our lives, we all get tired of being a puppet to everyone around us. We get tired of being a puppet to our emotions. When that moment comes in our lives where we no longer want to be controlled by everyone else (or even our own emotions), the first thing we have to do is learn how to stop being impulsively reactive.

Just the way you get good at everything you practice, you can equally get really good at pausing before you react impulsively. But it takes practice. The great news is, however, life will give you lots of opportunities to practice pausing (instead of reacting by lashing out impulsively). Pausing cannot fix impulsivity all by itself, though, so **it's important to understand that what you say to yourself when you pause matters.**

The next time you encounter a situation that drives you to wanting to lash out angrily or impulsively, practice pausing by saying to yourself, "I'm okay." The more you tell yourself that you're "okay" or "safe," the less your brain will send a message to throughout your body that you're in immediate danger. The "safer" you feel psychologically, the less likely you are to be reactive or impulsive.

The reality is that if you have experienced situations in your life where you really weren't safe or okay, then your brain probably got used to telling you that you needed to react impulsively and angrily to protect yourself. The challenge you now face, however, is teaching yourself how to distinguish between being in actual danger and just feeling like you're in danger. Of course, if you are in actual danger, then responding intensely to save yourself makes sense; but of course, if you are not in actual danger, then responding intensely or angrily is unnecessary.

EXERCISE:

1. What kinds of things tend to get you really angry, really quickly?

_____

_____

_____

_____

2. Describe ways that you have lashed out impulsively and unnecessarily aggressively in the past:

_____

_____

_____

_____

3. What types of every day situations can you begin to practice pausing and saying, "I'm okay," or "I'm safe"?

_____

_____

_____

_____

There is a difference between taking time to pause and just "trying to ignore" something. Being intentional about taking time to pause gives you an opportunity to practice being in control of your impulses, whereas sometimes just "trying to ignore" something can end up with you feeling more upset about it later on. Stuffing things down without actively working on them is rarely a good idea; on the other hand, practicing not reacting impulsively every time you feel angry is probably a very good idea.

Here are examples of different ways to handle the exact same situation. The more you recognize that there are always multiple ways to handle the same situation, the better chance you give yourself to pause when tough situations arise.

Situation	Self-talk	Consequence
Someone says something rude	"I can't stand it!"	Anger / Lashing out
Someone says something rude	"I'm okay. I'm safe."	You are in control of you

In the space below, give an example of situations that might come up, what you can say to yourself, and what the consequence would likely be:

Situation	Self-talk	Consequence

"The more you practice pausing and telling yourself that you're "safe" or "okay," the more in control of yourself you will feel."

-Dr. Christian Conte

49

THE MISERY CONTEST

Once in a very strange land, there lived a group of people who would hold an annual Misery Contest. The misery contest was held to find a champion - and then that champion would be crowned "the most miserable." So day in and day out, the people of the land would complain. They would complain about this and complain about that. They would complain about everything they could. They really, really wanted everyone to know how miserable they were.

Like everyone in life, the people in this strange land felt pain on the inside that others couldn't see. But the people in this land didn't think it was "fair" that others couldn't see the pain they had on the inside, so they would complain about their misery constantly. The people in this strange land felt like if they could be miserable enough, then they could get others to feel sorry for them. They believed that the more they could get others to feel sorry for them, the more they would be able to connect with others (and maybe even get what they want).

What the people of this land didn't know, however, is that by celebrating misery, they were only reinforcing it. In other words, the more they complained of their misery, the more others around them would complain of their misery, and the more others complained of their misery, the more the people continued to look for things to be miserable about…. And as you might have guessed, with all this focus on misery, it really was an awful place to live. But more than that: **The people who complained of their misery** really weren't getting others to feel sorry for them, in fact, they **were only pushing others away**. (Miserable people, of course, are always selfishly focused on themselves, whereas kind people tend to recognize that everyone struggles, and that life comes down to the attitude that we take toward it.)

For the people of this land, being miserable was a badge of honor, so even though it was their own attitude that was making them miserable, the people who lived in misery rarely wanted to leave. Now there were other places to go besides this land of misery: Beautiful lands filled with kind, friendly people who lived in gratitude - but still, the people in the land of misery rarely left, because misery was all they knew. Whereas the people in the land of misery only pushed others away with their negativity, the people everywhere else would gain more and more great connections with others, simply by being kind and grateful for all they had.

Sometimes the simplest answers (for example, "Live in gratitude and your life will be better") are the most difficult to begin practicing.

Avoiding the Land of Misery

You cannot control what others say and do, but you can always control what you say and do. The more you practice being grateful for everything you have, the more you will improve the attitude you have toward life. For better or worse, the reality is that people are more willing to help those who have a good attitude than they are to help someone with a poor attitude. Misery might love company, but people do not want to keep the company of those who have a miserable attitude.

All people suffer. All people experience internal struggles that others cannot fully understand. That is why constantly complaining about misery is selfish, negative, and tends to push others away. Just as you do not enjoy the company of those who are selfish, others do not (and will not) enjoy your company if or when you are being selfish.

Self-awareness is the key to recognizing if you are living in the "land of misery" or not.

1. What do you tend to complain about the most?

_____

_____

2. What can you do to minimize the amount of complaining you do?

_____

_____

3. Your focus determines your attitude. The more you focus on gratitude, the less you will focus on misery. What kinds of things can you be grateful about at all times in your life?

_____

_____

_____

_____

_____

"The more grateful you are, the less miserable you will be."

50

PRACTICING PEACE

By now, you have learned that whatever you practice, you master, and whatever you do every day is something you practice. You are a body, mind and spirit being, and it is important that you take care of all three aspects to yourself every day. You cannot eat once a week, for example, and expect to have a healthy body. Likewise, you cannot exercise once a week and expect to be physically fit. Finally, you cannot avoid feeding your spirit, and then expect that your spirit will somehow be magically fulfilled. Whatever you want, you have to practice.

The more clear you are with what you want, the more likely you are to get what you want. Peace is the ultimate goal for all of us, and the reality is, peace is achievable. You might not be able to control your external circumstances in life, but as you have seen all throughout this workbook: You alone are in control of your vast inner world. In the exercise below, make your goals for pursuing peace as clear as possible.

The more you can figure out, too, what might get in the way of you pursuing peace, the better chance you have to get around that obstacle. So it's important to not only identify what you want and how you'll go after it, but also what might come up to stop you, and what you can do to get around that, as well. The more prepared you are for what each day brings, the more effectively you will handle each day.

1. Today, I will practice peace physically by doing:

_____

_____

_____

_____

2. Today, I will practice peace mentally by reading / learning:

_____

_____

_____

_____

3. Today, I will practice peace spiritually by:

_____

_____

_____

_____

4. The biggest obstacles that can get in the way of me taking care of my body, mind and spirit are:

Body obstacle:

_____

Mind obstacle:

_____

Spirit obstacle:

_____

What I can do to get around these obstacles is:

_____

_____

_____

_____

And at the end of specific set of time, the student looked at the teacher, smiled and said:

"Thus, I have learned: What I practice, I will master. If I want peace, I have to practice peace. I am strong and capable and able. I am ready to practice pursuing the peace I hope to find. I will exercise my body in any way that I am capable of doing. I will strengthen my mind by only filling my mind with the type of things that I want to be in my mind. I will take care of my spirit by meditating and/or praying. What I practice, I will master. And I am ready to practice."

And she *was* ready. And so that's exactly what she did….

51

TWO PEOPLE

Once there were two people who lived in the same place. One person was **humble**, **compassionate** and **kind**, the other person was **arrogant**, **entitled** and **mean**.

Both people had difficult lives and both were in a very difficult situation. Both people struggled from time to time. Both people experienced tough emotions. But ***both people reacted very differently to everything that they experienced***.

When the humble, compassionate, kind person experienced hurt inside, she would let someone know about the tough time she was having. And even though it wasn't easy for her to go through tough times, she never felt entitled to make others suffer, as well. When she wanted something, she would ask for it in a kind way, but she never expected to get everything she asked for – so in the times where she did get what she asked for, she was very grateful; but if she was told "no," she was mature about accepting that.

When the arrogant, entitled, mean person experienced hurt inside, she felt like she *should* make others hurt, too – so she would lash out at others. When she wanted something, she *demanded* it from people (she was like a very spoiled, entitled child). If she got what she wanted, she said nothing (because she felt she was owed whatever she wanted). If she didn't get what she wanted/demanded, then she would scream and yell and threaten others. She acted very immaturely.

Questions to Consider:

1. Both people had troubled pasts and were in tough situations now, so why is it that each of them could respond so differently?

_____

_____

_____

_____

2. Of the two people, who would you rather be around? (Explain your answer)

_____

_____

_____

_____

3. Selfish children believe they are entitled to get whatever they want, and they feel entitled to say and do hurtful things to others. Selfish children minimize the harmful things they do, and they play the victim when they are caught doing wrong. **Why do you think they do that**, and **what is the best way to help them learn a better path**?

_____

_____

_____

_____

_____

_____

_____

_____

52

IT'S YOUR FAULT!

Once there lived a Blame Fish who blamed every other creature in the sea for everything he did. For example, he woke up feeling agitated one day, and as soon as he got up and felt like that, he swam by a lobster and yelled at the lobster, saying, "It's your fault I feel like this!" But the lobster knew it wasn't her fault that the Blame fish was feeling agitated. She knew it.

Then the Blame fish then swam past a school of smaller fish and when he did, he bumped into a rock, and then he screamed at the smaller fish, "It's your fault I swam into that rock because I was looking at you!" But even the smaller, younger fish knew that they didn't make the Blame fish look at them. They knew it.

The Blame fish then got a cramp in his side, and around the same time he got that cramp, he swam past a turtle. He snapped at the turtle, "It's your fault I have a cramp in my side!" But the turtle knew he didn't cause the Blame fish to have a cramp in his side. He knew it.

The Blame fish spent his whole life telling others that they were the cause of everything that was wrong in his life. He believed that as long as he could blame everyone else for what he said and did, then he wouldn't have to own responsibility for his words and actions – but here's the thing that everyone in the entire sea knew: The Blame fish was completely responsible for everything he said in did in life, just like they were. Just like everyone is.

We are all completely responsible for everything we say and do in life. Even if we feel agitated or irritable and don't know why – we are still entirely responsible for our thoughts, words, and actions.

The Blame fish was silly when he blamed others for things he chose to say and do. The harsh reality was that all the other fish in the ocean knew too, that he was silly when he blamed them for everything he said and did. You see, as much as he didn't think things were "fair," the real truth was that it wasn't fair for him to blame everyone else for the things he chose to say and do. In life, we are not always responsible for what happens to us in life, but we are all (the Blame fish included) completely responsible for everything we think, say and do.

EXERCISE:

Give an example of a time when others blamed you for their actions:

_____

_____

_____

_____

Give an example of a time when you blamed others for your actions:

_____

_____

_____

_____

What benefit do people get from blaming others for their actions?

_____

_____

_____

_____

What is the problem with blaming others for your own thoughts and actions?

_____

_____

_____

_____

You alone are responsible for you.

DAILY SCHEDULE

Wake up

Express gratitude

Meditate

Exercise

Read

Eat healthily

Do something kind for others

Give positive energy to the world

Be aware that others are seeing my actions, not my intentions

Take responsibility for my part in every communication I have

Think about my legacy and the bigger picture

Eat healthily

Meditate

Write

Encourage others

Share my talents with others

Practice / role-model loving-kindness

Express more gratitude

Get to sleep at a reasonable time

"There is only one today. Give your best to it."

- Dr. Christian Conte

YIELD THEORY OVERVIEW

The three core actions of Yield Theory are:

- Listen

- Validate

- Explore options

The seven fundamental components of Yield Theory are:

- Acceptance

- Authenticity

- Compassion

- Conscious Education

- Creativity

- Mindfulness

- Nonattachment

For more on Yield Theory, visit

www.DrChristianConte.com

www.YouTube.com/DrChristianConte

or see:

Conte, C. (2019). *Walking Through Anger: A New Design for Confronting Conflict in an Emotionally Charged World.* Sounds True Publishing. Louisville, CO.

THE AUTHOR

Dr. Christian Conte is a licensed professional counselor, level - V anger management specialist, author and professional speaker. He specializes in working with people convicted of violent crimes. He works with inmates, officers, and all levels of criminal justice personnel to implement effective communication strategies. Dr. Conte is the creator of Yield Theory, a model of communication rooted in compassion and conscious education. Yield Theory is used in organizations, prisons, and with sports teams throughout the world to transform both individuals and entire systems.

Made in the USA
San Bernardino, CA
10 November 2019